Profitable Letting

Fourmat Publishing

Profitable Letting
How to be a successful landlord

by Robert B Davies, Solicitor
and Diana Adie, Barrister

London
Fourmat Publishing
1989

ISBN 1 85190 080 2

First published 1989

All rights reserved

Published by Fourmat Publishing
27 & 28 St Albans Place, Islington Green, London N1 0NX

Typeset by Pentacor Ltd, High Wycombe, Bucks

Printed in Great Britain by Billing & Sons Ltd, Worcester

Preface

Before the 1914–18 war, ninety per cent of homes were rented from private landlords, but this proportion has been in steady decline ever since. While it is impossible to identify any single cause for this, there has been unprecedented interference by governments in the relationship between landlords and tenants over the last seventy years, mainly through the Rent Acts.

The previous edition of this book (*A Layman's Guide to Profitable Letting*, by Robert B. Davies) took a practical look at letting property under the 1977 Rent Act. There is now a new Act, the Housing Act 1988, which was passed with the intention of making it easier for private landlords to let their property. While it is too early to see whether the new Act will achieve its aim of transforming the rented housing market, the changes which it introduces are so dramatic that it was felt that an entirely new book was required.

This book aims to help prospective landlords avoid some of the most obvious pitfalls of letting property under the new Act. The new legislation is complex and it must be remembered that no book of law for the layman can ever take the place of proper legal advice. It is *always* advisable to take legal advice before letting property and to get a tenancy agreement drawn up by a lawyer. However, this book may help landlords to understand something of the structure of the new law and to realise the limits of what they can and cannot do in relation to their tenants. The other main objective is to give landlords practical advice about letting property.

Chapter 1 gives a summary of the present law as contained in the Housing Act 1988, and a basic outline of the legal responsibilities of landlord and tenant. Although the Housing Act aims to simplify the law, it is not easy to read or understand. Basically, under the Housing

Act a landlord has the choice between letting on an assured tenancy or an assured shorthold tenancy. The let can be at a market rent (which cannot be reduced), where the tenant has a right to remain in the premises so long as he or she performs his obligations under the tenancy; or the let can be for a fixed time to a tenant who will have no right to remain in the property after the letting ends, but who can apply to have the rent reduced.

Chapter 2 sets out the types of letting available to the landlord who does not wish to risk having sitting tenants in the property. Briefly, any person who wishes to let property which he does not occupy himself has the option of either a holiday or company let, or else a letting under the Housing Act. The appropriate form of letting will depend on the circumstances of the owner and of the property. For example, the Act provides that an owner temporarily living away from home can let the property on an assured tenancy and recover possession after the term of the tenancy has expired, so long as he gives notice to the tenant in proper form. Similarly, the owner of a holiday cottage can let it out of season providing the correct notices are given.

Alternatively, a landlord can let on an assured shorthold tenancy for a period of at least six months and will be certain of regaining possession if the correct notices have been served.

Chapter 3 gives practical advice on how to arrange a letting. This includes setting up the premises; ways of finding and selecting a tenant; the use of managing agents and the preparation of a tenancy agreement.

Chapter 4 deals with the ever-increasing market for holiday cottages. It covers the legal position of holiday lets together with the various considerations involved in preparing a cottage for letting. In addition there is a section on marketing the property, and extensive advice about converting premises for letting as holiday cottages.

Farm cottages may be used for holiday letting but are still frequently occupied by agricultural workers, and the special regime which applies to these occupants is dealt with in Chapter 5. The Housing Act has made some changes to the existing legislation in this area but it preserves the rights of farm workers and their families to continue in occupation of property even when their employment with a particular farmer has ended.

An area of more general interest is covered in Chapter 6 where the law applicable to householders who let rooms in their own homes is set out. While these types of letting tend to cause fewer legal problems, the practical implications of having tenants in your own home need to be seriously considered. There is also a section on the increasing tendency for landlords to let to homeless DSS claimants, and the potentially difficult consequences of these lets.

Chapter 7 deals with the taxation of rented property, both furnished and unfurnished. It looks at Capital Gains Tax and Inheritance Tax in relation to rented property and gives various practical examples.

Finally, there are some words of warning in Chapter 8: the do's and don'ts of letting property, and advice when things go wrong.

For the sake of brevity and simplicity, the landlord is usually referred to in the text as "he", "him" and "his"; no discrimination is intended!

This book deals with the law as contained in the Housing Act 1988. Due to the current absence of judicial authority or interpretation of many of the Act's provisions, the purpose of the book can be to serve as a basic guide only. As already stated above, readers are recommended always to seek legal advice when embarking on letting property.

We are indebted to Steve Smith, partner with Murphy Salisbury & Co, Chartered Accountants, Stratford-upon-Avon, for his considerable assistance with Chapter 7.

We would also like to thank Michael Soole and Caroline Hutton for their constructive advice and comments on the text.

RBD
DA
April 1989

Contents

General principles

The last twenty years have seen a huge reduction in the proportion of rented property in Britain. Some of this is due to the great modern enthusiasm for home-ownership, but the change has also been encouraged by the massive and far-reaching legislation contained in the Rent Acts. The most recent of these was the 1977 Rent Act (itself amended by the Housing Act 1980), which many landlords felt discriminated against them, and tilted the balance too far towards the rights of tenants.

We now have a new Housing Act, which came into effect on 15 January 1989. The aims of the new Act are to make it simpler for landlords to let property at a market rent, and to recover possession when the tenancy comes to an end. However, the new Act is not a landlord's charter, and it has to be used with care if a landlord wishes to let profitably, and still be able to regain possession when he wants to. It is also important to remember that the Housing Act 1988 only applies to *new* lettings; existing tenants still have the protection of the Rent Acts.

Before anyone considers letting property of any kind, it is vital to understand the basis of the obligations as landlords, and the rights of tenants under the law. Landlords who enter into letting agreements without first bothering to find out what the law is, may find that they end up with a property occupied by sitting tenants who cannot be evicted, and whose presence devalues the property. Landlords who do find out what the law says, and realise the limits of what they can and cannot do, can avoid falling into the many traps which await the unwary.

The new Act has not affected the basic legal concepts that apply to dealings between landlords and tenants involved in letting residential property. They are:

- protection from eviction;
- security of tenure;
- tenancy or licence.

These three concepts are the key to understanding how the law weighs up the often conflicting rights and obligations of landlords and tenants.

1. Protection from eviction

All occupiers of residential property are entitled to a degree of protection from being evicted from their homes, whether they live in a house or a single furnished room. It is a criminal offence to use force, or the threat of force, to gain entry to premises, even when the occupants are there without the landlord's consent, as in the case of squatters. In other words, if the occupiers of property do not leave peacefully when asked to do so, the landlord cannot evict them himself. He must bring proceedings in the local county court and obtain an order for possession.

If the landlord fails to do this and harasses an occupant into leaving, he may be guilty of a criminal offence. An occupant who has been forced to leave in this way may also have a claim for very substantial damages and an injunction which will force the landlord to allow him back into the property.

With a few exceptions (known as *excluded* tenancies and licences) all residential occupiers are also entitled to a minimum of four weeks' written notice to leave premises. This notice has to be in a particular form and unless this *prescribed* form is used a landlord will be unable to bring possession proceedings successfully. In many cases it will be necessary to give more than four weeks' written notice to a tenant, but it is important to remember that a landlord will nearly always have to give at least four weeks' notice.

2. Security of tenure

Many occupiers of residential property are also entitled to a further degree of protection from being evicted from their homes, called security of tenure. It means that when the landlord applies to the court for an order for possession, this will only be granted in certain specified circumstances. Whether or not the court decides to give the property back to the landlord, depends on whether the landlord can prove one of the so-called "grounds for possession", laid down by the Housing Act. If the landlord cannot establish a "ground for possession", the occupier will be entitled to stay in the property for as long as he wishes, as a sitting tenant. Although the landlord will continue to be paid rent by the tenant, the court will not give the property back to him until he can establish a "ground for possession".

3. Tenancy or licence?

There is a very important difference between an occupier of property who has a *licence*, and one who has a *tenancy*. By and large, a licensee does not have security of tenure, while a tenant does.

The granting of a licence does not give the occupier any interest in the property, but merely a right to use and live in it, or part of it. Typical examples of licensees are people who occupy a hotel bedroom for the night, or guests who come to stay. On the other hand, a tenant is someone who is entitled to what is known as *exclusive possession* of a part of the property. This means that the tenant has a right to occupy the particular part of the premises alone and can exclude anyone else from it if he wishes.

In many cases it is very difficult to tell whether a person is actually a tenant or a licensee. Some parts of the law are still not at all clear, particularly where there are several occupiers sharing a flat or house. This was recently demonstrated in two flat-sharing cases decided by the House of Lords, where in both cases the agreements stated that the occupiers were licensees and not entitled to exclusive possession.

Despite this, when the court looked at the facts, it decided that in one case the occupiers were joint tenants, while the others only had a licence.

Although both tenants and licensees are protected from eviction, the fact that only tenants can have security of tenure has led to attempts by many landlords to avoid the protection of the legislation by calling what is really a tenancy a licence or exclusive licence. The message that has come out of recent court cases, including those mentioned above, is that no matter what the parties call the agreement, whether a lease, licence or whatever, the court will look at the intention of the parties to see what has actually been created.

In one of the leading cases on this point it was decided that although the agreement described itself as a licence, it was on its true interpretation a lease, and the tenant consequently enjoyed security of tenure. The judge went on to make clear the very important principle that the relationship between the parties is decided by law and not by the label which the parties choose to put on it. It is a matter of ascertaining the true relationship of the parties.

This can have very important repercussions for landlords, and to illustrate the point it is worth looking at the case of *Street* v. *Mountford* which was decided by the House of Lords in 1985. The facts of the case were as follows: Mr. Roger Street entered into an agreement with Mrs. Wendy Mountford, under which she occupied furnished rooms for £37 per week, at 5, St. Clements Gardens, Bournemouth. Mr. Street was not resident, but let out other rooms in the same building.

The written agreement between the two parties was called a "licence", and the money payable by Mrs. Mountford was called a "licence fee". The document was signed by both parties, and concluded with the statements, "I understand and accept that a licence in the above form does not and is not intended to give me a tenancy protected under the Rent Acts". This clause was also signed by Mrs. Mountford.

So far as the law was concerned, the most important part of this document was a provision which read, "the owner (or his agent) has the right at all times to enter the rooms and to inspect their condition, read and collect money from meters, carry out maintenance works, install or replace furniture or for any other reasonable purpose". The court felt that since Mr. Street expressly reserved this right, it followed that the remainder of the "licence" granted exclusive possession to Mrs. Mountford.

When the case went to the House of Lords, it was stated in their judgment that although the document was called a "licence", the circumstances suggested otherwise, and Mrs. Mountford was entitled to a tenancy, and therefore protection under the Rent Act. If a landlord let his property in these circumstances today, he would probably find that Mrs. Mountford was an assured tenant under the Housing Act and entitled to its protection.

The result was that Mr. Street could not evict Mrs. Mountford, as she was a protected Rent Act tenant. She had applied to the rent officer for a fair rent to be registered and in view of the circumstances the rent officer reduced the rent agreed from £37 to only £14 per week. What may have been a fair rent to Mrs. Mountford may have seemed a little unfair to Mr. Street, particularly as he also had a property considerably devalued by the presence of a sitting tenant.

The judge in the case stated that if the agreement satisfied all the requirements of a tenancy, the parties cannot alter its effect by insisting that they had only created a licence. Using a rather apt analogy he went on to say, ". . . the manufacture of a five-pronged implement for manual digging results in a fork even if the manufacturer, unfamiliar with the English language, insists that he intended to make and has made a spade . . ."

The moral of the story is that it is clearly unsafe to enter into a licence agreement where the landlord is not resident in the building. This is the same whether the Rent Act or the Housing Act applies, although it should be said that a tenancy granted under the Housing Act today would not allow the likes of Mrs. Mountford to seek what was known as a fair rent.

However, the recent flat-sharing cases already mentioned have confirmed that it *is* possible to let premises on a licence in certain circumstances where a number of people are sharing the whole of the property. A landlord who is considering letting a house or flat to a number of individuals such as students may be able to let on licence, depending on the particular circumstances. This should *not* be done without taking legal advice as it is a very difficult area and special agreements would have to be drawn up.

4. Rent Act or Housing Act?

The Housing Act 1988 came into effect on 15 January 1989 and applies to new lettings only. Anyone who let property before that date will not be covered by the Housing Act and in all probability their tenants will be protected by the Rent Act 1977. It is not the aim of this book to explain the rights of existing tenants, and if a landlord has tenants who are paying a fair or registered rent, or were in possession before 15 January 1989, he should take legal advice before taking any steps. Landlords who let their property on shorthold tenancies before 15 January 1989 should refer to page 30 to check the status of their tenants.

There are three other circumstances where a tenancy will not be covered by the Housing Act and these are:

(1) where the landlord agreed to let the property to the tenant and that agreement was made before 15 January 1989 (in which case the provisions of the Rent Act 1977 may well apply);

(2) if the tenant was previously the tenant of other property belonging to the landlord and the landlord obtained a court order for possession of the property on the basis that the tenant would be provided with other accommodation;

(3) if the landlord grants the tenancy to one of his existing Rent Act tenants.

The main difference between tenancies which come under the Rent Act and those under the Housing Act is that Rent Act tenancies are subject to a complex system of rent control which allows the tenant to have a *fair* rent registered; a fair rent may be much lower than the *market* rent. A Rent Act tenant also has a higher degree of security of tenure than a Housing Act tenant, but in both cases the tenant is entitled to remain in possession until the landlord obtains a court order and this will be granted only in certain specified circumstances.

The Housing Act 1988 applies to all tenancies entered into after 15 January 1989. The main type of tenancy which the Act creates is called an *assured tenancy* and its purpose is to allow the tenant to have security of tenure while enabling the landlord to charge a market rent. Once the landlord and tenant have agreed the rent it will not generally be altered until the landlord decides to increase it. The tenant then has a right to apply to a rent assessment committee which will fix a rent that is supposed to reflect the open market rent for the property.

Four categories of tenancy are dealt with by the Act:

1. tenancies which are not assured;
2. assured tenancies;
3. assured shorthold tenancies;
4. assured agricultural occupancies.

5. Tenancies which are not assured

The Act states that certain lettings will not be assured tenancies and therefore do not fall within the Act's regime of security of tenure and limited rent control. The most important of these is a tenancy or tenancy agreement which was made before 15 January 1989. While this does not mean that such tenancies have *no* protection, they are not covered by the 1988 Act. Apart from pre-existing tenancies, the other types of letting which are *not* assured tenancies are:

- lettings to a company;
- tenancies of a property where the rateable value exceeds £1,500 in Greater London or £750 elsewhere;
- tenancies at no rent or at a rent which is lower than two thirds of the rateable value of the property at the time;
- tenancies of property which is used wholly or partly for a business or which is licensed premises;
- tenancies of agricultural holdings or where more than two acres of agricultural land is let with the property;
- tenancies granted by certain educational institutions to students;
- holiday lettings;
- tenancies of property where the landlord is resident on the premises and has always owned and occupied the house or flat as his only or principal home, *except* where the landlord occupies another flat in a purpose-built block of flats;
- tenancies where the landlord is a local authority or government department.

The types of "non-assured tenancy" that are most likely to appeal to private landlords are holiday lets, company lets and lettings by resident landlords, since these are the simplest ways of ensuring that a tenant does not have security of tenure. If a tenancy falls into any of the categories listed above the tenant will not have security of tenure, but he will be entitled to protection from eviction. Unless the tenancy is for a fixed term, the landlord can bring it to an end only by serving on the tenant a notice which is called a "notice to quit". This must be in a prescribed form. If the tenant does not leave, the landlord will have to apply to the court for an order for possession.

6. Assured tenancies

(a) Security of tenure

If a tenancy is granted after 15 January 1989 and does not fall within any of the categories already mentioned, it is an assured tenancy and the landlord will only be able to obtain an order for possession on certain grounds. It does not matter that there is no written agreement. Whether the tenancy is of a single room, a whole house or a flat; furnished or unfurnished, the tenant will still have security of tenure.

This will be the case whether the tenancy is granted for a fixed term – six months, a year, three years, for example; or for an indefinite period where the tenant simply continues in occupation paying rent on a weekly, monthly, quarterly or annual basis. The second type of letting is known as a periodic tenancy and it continues to exist until either the tenant leaves or a court order is made.

When a fixed term tenancy comes to an end (unless the tenant himself terminates it), the tenant is allowed to remain in occupation on the same terms as before, but for an indefinite period; and he is now known as a *statutory periodic tenant*. So if a landlord has let his property for, say, three years, at the end of the three year period a new type of tenancy automatically arises and continues indefinitely until either a court order is obtained by the landlord, or the tenant leaves of his own accord. There is a special procedure for fixing a new rent and new terms of the tenancy in these circumstances, and this is explained later in the chapter (see page 16).

If the landlord tries to evict the tenant without a court order, or harasses him into leaving, he may be guilty of a criminal offence under the Protection from Eviction Act 1977. He can also find that the tenant has a claim for very substantial damages against him. It is important to remember that this applies to any residential occupier, whether a licensee or tenant, and if in doubt it is always safer to take legal advice and then apply to the court for an order, rather than risk prosecution and an injunction or damages.

(b) Grounds for recovery of possession

If a tenant does refuse to leave at the end of a tenancy, the landlord should always consult a solicitor first. There are three steps to regaining possession:

- notice of proceedings for possession;
- issue of possession proceedings;
- court order.

The landlord must first serve a notice on the tenant. The notice has to be in the prescribed form, and states that the landlord intends to begin possession proceedings within a certain time (see Appendix 1). It also tells the tenant the Ground on which the landlord is seeking possession, and particulars of that Ground. Once the period of time specified in the notice has expired, the next step is to apply to the local county court to issue possession proceedings. Finally, if the tenant has still not left, the landlord will have to go to court to obtain an order for possession.

The court will only make an order for possession on one of the Grounds which are listed in Schedule 2 to the Act. This is divided into two parts:

Part I contains Grounds on which the court *must* order possession. This means that so long as the landlord can prove that the facts of his case fall within one of these Grounds he will be granted an order for possession.

Part II contains Grounds on which the court *may* order possession. If the court is satisfied that any of the Grounds in Part II is established then it has a *discretion* to make an order if it considers it reasonable to do so. In practice this means that even when a tenant has broken an obligation of the tenancy, for instance by sub-letting the property, the court may still refuse to grant an order for possession.

Where a tenant has failed to pay rent, this can be either a Part I or Part II Ground. There are three possibilities; a tenant can be consistently late in paying his rent; he can owe some rent; or he can owe a large amount of rent. The first two examples are Part II Grounds, and it is common for a court to make a "suspended" possession order which allows the tenant to remain in possession so long as he pays the rent, and a certain amount off any rent arrears. If a tenant owes more than a specified amount of rent, then the court *must* order possession.

The court also has very wide powers in a Part II Ground to either adjourn possession proceedings or postpone the date for possession for as long as it likes on terms that the tenant pays the rent and complies with other conditions the court wishes to impose. At the end of the period the court may decide to discharge the possession order altogether if it is satisfied with the tenant's conduct in the meantime. This can lead to long periods of uncertainty for the landlord, and it illustrates the advantages of the Part I Grounds, where possession *must* be ordered.

PART I: GROUNDS WHERE POSSESSION MUST BE ORDERED

Ground 1: Owner-occupiers

There are two situations where landlords who let property which has been or will be their home are entitled to possession. Provided that the landlord has always owned the property and did not purchase a part-occupied house, he will be able to recover possession if he has either lived in the property as his only or principal home at some time before the tenancy was granted, or if he needs the property now as an only or principal home for himself or his spouse. In both cases he must also have served a written notice on the tenant, before or at the time the tenancy was granted, that possession would be recovered on this Ground. The notice requirement is really essential even though in certain circumstances the court has a discretion to dispense with it.

Ground 2: Mortgaged property

Where the property was mortgaged *before* the tenancy was granted and the bank or building society wishes to take possession of the property or sell it, the court will order possession if the tenant was given notice of this in the same way as in Ground 1. Again, the court can dispense with notice if it thinks it fair in the circumstances.

Ground 3: Out of season lets for holiday property
An owner of property which is normally let for holiday purposes can also let it for up to eight months for non-holiday purposes. The property must have been let for holiday purposes within the twelve months immediately before commencement of the tenancy, and the tenancy itself has to be for a fixed term of eight months or less. It is essential that a written notice is given to the tenant on or before the commencement of the tenancy. For further details see Chapter 2, and the form of notice required is given in Appendix 1.

Ground 4: Lettings out of the student term
This enables specified educational institutions to grant tenancies of up to twelve months where, in the previous twelve months, the property had been let to students and proper notice has been served. A private landlord who lets to students is *not* covered by this Ground.

Ground 5: Parsonage houses
Where a house is owned for the purpose of occupation by a minister of religion as a residence for him from which to perform his duties and is required for this purpose, possession can be recovered provided tenants are given written notice.

Ground 6: Demolition or reconstruction
A landlord who acquired his interest in the property before the tenancy was granted, or a subsequent landlord who did not purchase the property (for example, someone who inherited the property), with the *assured* tenant in occupation, can obtain possession to carry out certain works to the property. The works must be substantial or involve the demolition or reconstruction of the whole or a substantial part of the property; and it must be necessary to have possession in order to carry out the works. Before he seeks an order for possession the landlord must ensure that, if practicable, he gives the tenant the option of either occupying a smaller part of the property or of allowing access to enable the works to be carried out. In the case of registered housing associations or housing trusts this Ground applies if their superior landlord wishes to demolish or reconstruct the property.

Ground 7: Death of the tenant
On a tenant's death his tenancy may pass to someone else, either by will, on intestacy (no will), or by a statutory right of succession to a member of his family who was also living in the property. The statutory

right of succession is a complex area and is dealt with briefly at page 14.
If there is no statutory right of succession and the old tenant had a
periodic tenancy, the landlord is entitled to possession provided he
starts proceedings within twelve months of the old tenant's death.
Although the landlord can accept rent from the new tenant without
prejudicing his right to possession he must *not* make any agreement
with him or alter the terms of the tenancy. This is not an easy situation
and when a tenant dies it is important to take legal advice immediately
as to what should be done.

Ground 8: Non-payment of rent
Where the tenant is in arrears with his rent and the arrears exceed
specified amounts both at the time the landlord serves notice seeking
possession *and* at the date of the hearing, possession must be ordered.
The amounts which must be unpaid vary depending on when rent is
usually paid:

(a) if rent is paid weekly or fortnightly, at least thirteen weeks' rent
must be unpaid;
(b) if monthly, at least three months' rent must be unpaid;
(c) if quarterly, at least one quarter's rent must be more than three
months overdue;
(d) if yearly, at least three months' rent must be more than three
months overdue.

This is an important Ground and it means that if the tenant does not
pay the amount of rent due by the date of the court hearing the landlord
will be granted possession. However, it is always possible that the
tenant will pay off all or some of the rent arrears on the day of the
hearing, and the court would then have a discretion whether or not to
make an order.

PART II: GROUNDS WHERE POSSESSION MAY BE ORDERED

Ground 9: suitable alternative accommodation is or will be made
available for the tenant either by the local authority who can provide a
certificate to this effect (although this rarely happens in practice), or by
the landlord.

Ground 10: the tenant is in arrears with some of his rent, both at the
date when notice seeking possession is served and when proceedings are
begun.

Ground 11: the tenant has persistently delayed paying rent.

Ground 12: the tenant has broken any obligation of the tenancy other than the obligation to pay rent.

Ground 13: the tenant or anyone living with him has allowed the condition of any part of the property which he uses to deteriorate.

Ground 14: the tenant or anyone living with him has caused nuisance or annoyance to adjoining occupiers or has been convicted of using the property or allowing it to be used for immoral or illegal purposes.

Ground 15: the tenant or anyone living with him has allowed the condition of furniture in the property to deteriorate.

Ground 16: the tenant occupied the property as a result of his employment by the landlord or a previous landlord and he has ceased to be in that employment.

In the case of a periodic tenancy or a fixed term tenancy which has expired, the landlord can rely on any of the Grounds set out in the Act. But where a fixed term tenancy has not yet come to an end the Grounds available to the landlord are limited. He can only obtain possession on Grounds 2 or 8 and 10 to 15, and the tenancy agreement must also contain a provision allowing him to terminate the tenancy on the Ground in question.

(c) Recovering possession

If the landlord cannot recover possession on any of the sixteen Grounds outlined above, the tenant can remain in possession as a periodic tenant for as long as he wishes provided he pays rent at the same intervals as before and complies with all the obligations of the original tenancy. The tenant is not allowed to transfer his tenancy or sub-let any part of the property, and if a landlord discovers that there are new tenants in the property he should be careful not to accept any rent from them in case this is seen as recognising a new tenancy.

When an order for possession is granted it will usually take effect in twenty-eight days' time in order to give the tenant an opportunity to find accommodation, but where possession is given on a Part II Ground the court can give the tenant as much time as it likes. A landlord who has recovered possession on either the Ground of demolition or reconstruction of the property or the provision of alternative accommodation (Grounds 6 or 9) will have to pay the tenant's reasonable removal expenses.

Although local authorities have a duty to house unintentionally homeless people under the Housing (Homeless Persons) Act 1977, it is unlikely that any accommodation will be offered until a court order is made and taken to the housing department. If the tenant does not leave by the end of the time ordered for possession, the landlord may have to apply for a warrant from the court and eventually get the bailiff to evict the tenant.

(d) Succession to a tenancy

It has already been pointed out that on the death of a tenant it may not be possible to recover possession of property if there is a statutory right of succession. The Act allows the spouse or co-habitee of an assured *periodic* tenant to take over the tenancy, so long as the property was their only or principal home and they were living there immediately before the death of the tenant.

---

7. Assured shorthold tenancies

Assured shorthold is a completely new and a very important kind of tenancy. These tenancies will be referred to as "shortholds", but they should not be confused with any kind of shorthold tenancy that was granted before 15 January 1989. (For further information about the old shorthold tenancies granted under the Rent Act, see page 30). Shortholds are discussed in detail in Chapter 2 and share the same characteristics as assured tenancies except in two important respects:

(a) A shorthold tenant does not have security of tenure *provided* that the landlord has complied with the necessary formalities. In other words, at the end of the agreed term, if the tenant does not leave the property peacefully, the court *must* grant an order giving the landlord possession; and

(b) A shorthold tenant can apply to have the agreed rent reduced in certain circumstances.

8. Assured agricultural occupancies

These are dealt with in Chapter 5 and are only of interest to owners of farm cottages since they provide security of tenure for agricultural workers and their families.

9. Terms of the tenancy

It is always important that all the terms, particularly the rent, are agreed before the tenancy starts. These terms should be drafted with care to make sure all the landlord's requirements are covered, and embodied in a written tenancy agreement. In the case of an assured tenancy, the terms agreed by the parties will remain in force until either the parties agree to alter them or one of the following occurs:

(a) a fixed term tenancy comes to an end and the tenant remains in possession as a statutory periodic tenant;
(b) the landlord wishes to increase the rent of a periodic tenancy;
(c) there is an assured shorthold tenancy and the rent charged is significantly higher than the rent for other similar tenancies (see Chapter 2 for a discussion of rents in shortholds).

The procedure in each case varies, but all may involve an application to a rent assessment committee for a determination of the rent which could reasonably be charged by the landlord.

Where a fixed term tenancy has come to an end and the tenant is entitled to remain in possession as a statutory periodic tenant, both landlord and tenant have a right to vary the terms of the statutory periodic tenancy. This is done by serving a notice in the prescribed form (see Appendix 1, page 119), not later than one year after the tenancy ended. The notice must state the terms which either party proposes, and may also include an adjustment to the rent to take account of those terms. Once the notice has been served, either party has three months to refer it to a rent assessment committee. The committee will decide what terms should reasonably be included in the tenancy and what adjustment should be made to the rent.

If neither party refers the notice to a committee within the three month period, then the terms proposed in the notice become the terms of the tenancy and take effect on the date stated in the notice (although this must not be earlier than three months from the date the notice is served). Even though a notice has been referred to a committee, the parties can still agree what terms they wish to include in the tenancy and they can jointly withdraw the application from the committee by giving written notice.

Note that if a landlord only wants to increase the rent and not alter the terms he should follow the procedure set out below.

10. Increasing the rent

If the landlord decides to let his property on a periodic tenancy it is usually advisable to agree increases of rent in advance. For example, the tenancy agreement could provide that the rent will be increased by a certain amount after a year and again after two years and so on.

Where the parties have not made any arrangements in the original tenancy agreement for a higher rent to be paid after a certain period of time, or where there is a statutory periodic tenancy, a landlord who wants to increase the rent must first serve a notice on the tenant. The notice has to be in a prescribed form (see Appendix 1, page 119) and will propose a new rent as well as stating the date on which it is to take effect. There are limitations on when the new rent can begin and the date given in the notice must be:

(a) at least a year after the start of the tenancy; and
(b) at least a year after any previous increase in rent; and
(c) at least a month from the date of service of the notice where the tenancy is monthly or weekly, and at least six months for a yearly tenancy.

For any other type of periodic tenancy the amount of notice given must be the same as the period of the tenancy, for example, a quarter for a quarterly tenancy; three months for a three-monthly tenancy.

The new rent will take effect on the date stated by the landlord unless the tenant refers the notice to a rent assessment committee before that date, or the landlord and tenant agree different terms. Once the notice has been referred to the rent assessment committee the committee will determine a rent for the property which they consider to be a reasonable market rent, and will also decide when it is to take effect. It is always open to the landlord and tenant to reach some agreement on the rent rather than leaving it to the committee to decide, and if this happens they can withdraw the reference by giving the committee written notice. [The procedure whereby a shorthold tenant can apply to a rent assessment committee to have the rent reduced is described in Chapter 2.]

Although rent assessment committees have been in existence for a long time, the new Act changes their role and it is difficult at this stage to predict how the system will work in practice. Leaflets explaining the working of the committees together with application forms are available from local Citizen's Advice Bureaux, and the housing department of the local council can usually give practical advice.

11. Rates and rent books

Normally, rates are payable by the occupier of premises, but in the case of tenancies for a period of less than three months or where the rent is payable at less than quarterly intervals, the owner will be liable for the rates and cannot recover them from the tenant unless he has made provision for this in the tenancy agreement. Rates are not included in any determination by the rent assessment committee of the rent payable.

The Landlord and Tenant Act 1985 contains the provisions relating to when a rent book must be given to a tenant and the information it should contain. There is a strict duty on a landlord to provide a rent book where the rent is payable weekly, but not in cases where a substantial part of the rent is in respect of board. A rent book must contain the following information:

(a) the name and address of the landlord. If the landlord is a

company the tenant can request (and should be told) the names and addresses of all directors and the secretary;
(b) details of the rent and rates payable by the occupier;
(c) certain prescribed information relating to the tenant's rights to security of tenure (see Appendix 1, page 117).

Rent books with forms can be purchased from most large book shops or law stationers.

It should be noted that it is a criminal offence punishable by a fine (maximum £50 for the first offence) to fail to provide a rent book. If a rent book is not provided it does not affect the right of the landlord to recover the rent properly due to him from the tenant, but a well-kept rent book is a good record, and may be helpful in any court proceedings.

12. Landlord's repairing obligations

The landlord is obliged under the provisions of the Landlord and Tenant Act 1985 to be responsible for repairs to the structure and exterior of the house which he lets, which includes drains, gutters and exterior pipes. He will *always* be liable for these repairs provided that the lease is for a term of less than seven years. In addition, he must keep in repair and working order the installations of water, gas, electricity, sanitation (which includes basins, sink and baths), and also space heating and water heating. The tenant is of course under a duty to use the property in a tenant-like manner. Any attempt to make the tenant liable to repair or maintain any of the above installations is void and of no effect.

In deciding the standard of repair expected of the landlord, one has to have regard to the age, character, prospective life and locality of the property. If the tenant wishes the landlord to carry out repairs for which he (the landlord) is responsible then the tenant must inform him of any works necessary. These may include works to parts of the building which are not actually let to the tenant, if they are in disrepair and affect either the tenant's flat or any part of the building that the tenant is entitled to use.

In any tenancy where the landlord is obliged to carry out repairs he, or any person authorised by him, may enter the premises at reasonable times of the day on giving at least twenty-four hours' notice in writing to the occupier, for the purpose of viewing the condition and state of repair.

There are further implied terms of every assured tenancy that the tenant must allow the landlord access and all reasonable facilities for carrying out those repairs which the landlord is entitled to do.

It must be stressed that any attempt by the landlord to avoid his legal responsibilities, even by agreement with the tenant before commencement of the tenant's lease, would be void, and the landlord would still be responsible for the repairing obligations outlined above.

2

Choosing the best type of letting

Perhaps the greatest fear of most private landlords is that they will be unable to get their tenants to leave at the end of the letting, and that they will find themselves with sitting tenants in a property which they may wish to sell or use for some other purpose. To prevent this from happening, a landlord who wants to make sure that he can regain possession of his property has three alternatives:

- a letting which is not covered by the Housing Act 1988;
- an assured shorthold tenancy under the Housing Act 1988;
- an assured tenancy which comes within one of the Grounds set out in Part I of Schedule 2 to the Act where the court *must* grant an order for possession.

Any other tenancy which a landlord enters into will allow a tenant to remain in possession of the property for as long as he wishes, so long as he pays the rent and does not breach any of the terms of the tenancy agreement. A landlord will only be able to get possession of the property if he can rely on one of the Grounds in Part II of Schedule 2 to the Act, and this will be at the court's discretion.

1. Lettings which fall outside the Act

There are really only three types of letting which fall outside the Act and are suitable for most private landlords. These are holiday lets, company lets and lettings by resident landlords. If a landlord enters into a tenancy agreement which falls into any of these categories the Housing Act 1988 will not apply; the tenant will not be an assured tenant and will have neither security of tenure nor any right to have the rent altered by a rent assessment committee.

(a) Holiday lettings

If a property is let strictly for the purpose of a holiday, it is not covered by the Housing Act. But the letting must genuinely be for that sole purpose. A property owner wishing to let his property for short lets of weeks at a time usually does no more than exchange letters with prospective tenants, who will place a deposit for the weeks they wish to book the accommodation, and the owner confirms the booking. It is quite possible for a person (such as an overseas resident taking an extended holiday) to occupy a property for holiday purposes for several months, but the purpose of the letting must be a holiday.

If there is a written agreement between the parties stating that the letting is for the tenant's holiday, this will be evidence of the terms of the contract and will be taken into consideration if the matter ever goes to court. If, however, the agreement was a sham and the landlord knew at the time of the letting that it was not for holiday purposes, but an attempt to escape the provisions of the Act, then the landlord would have great difficulty in evicting the tenant. Unless the landlord could rely on another Ground for possession under the Act, the tenant would be able to remain in the property as an assured tenant. A court might, for example, be rather sceptical that a letting in an industrial area for a lengthy period was actually for the purpose of a holiday, whatever the parties agreed between themselves.

Holiday lettings are one of the exceptional cases known as "excluded tenancies" where it is not obligatory for a landlord to apply for a court order to evict a tenant who refuses to leave at the end of the letting. A holiday letting will normally be for a fixed period and if a tenant is still in occupation at the end of this time he should be asked to leave, and if he refuses, the police should be called if necessary. As it is an offence to use force to evict a tenant, where a tenant refuses to leave the premises peacefully, it is best to consult a solicitor and possession proceedings may have to be brought.

(b) Company lettings

A letting where the tenant is a company rather than an individual is also excluded from the protection of the Housing Act. It can be a useful form of tenancy for a private landlord who wishes to obtain a good return from his property without the risk of creating an assured tenancy, but the landlord must beware of a "sham" – for example where the person occupying the property takes responsibility for paying the rent and the company is not really involved at all.

Since a company itself cannot actually occupy property, what a company let means in practice is that a tenancy agreement will be made with a company, which then houses one or more of its officers or employees in the property as licensees.

There are a number of drawbacks to company lets and these are as follows:

(a) The company itself is responsible for paying the rent, so care should be taken to ensure that it is one of substance, and not merely a "paper" company without proper funding.

(b) It may be difficult to keep track of who is actually occupying the property, and problems could arise over sub-letting.

(c) The occupiers of the property, who will be company employees, have no interest in the property themselves. They may therefore be less concerned about looking after the property, or may even refuse to leave if they cease to be employed by the company.

For these reasons it is probably wise to use a letting agency or managing agents (see Chapter 3) for company lets, as agents are familiar with this type of letting and can inspect the property regularly on the landlord's behalf. It is also best to let to large, established companies to avoid any problems over recovery of rent, and it is vital that a proper tenancy agreement is prepared.

An agreement should contain certain clauses which will protect the landlord against most foreseeable problems. These will include a surety clause making one of the directors of the company personally liable for payment of the rent and for any damage which occurs to the property. This will enable a landlord to sue the director for any losses if the company goes into liquidation or fails to pay the rent.

There should also be a clause stating that the company can only allow its officers or employees to occupy the property as licensees, and any breach of the clause will entitle the landlord to repossess the property. Rent should normally be paid by the company directly and if a landlord discovers that the occupiers of the property are not company employees he should take legal advice immediately and should on no account accept rent from the occupiers, as this may prevent him from recovering possession.

It is also a good idea to put a clause in the tenancy agreement allowing the landlord to inspect the property at regular intervals, and this right should be exercised to keep an eye on the condition of the premises and the occupiers. All these clauses will be standard in any properly drawn tenancy agreement.

(c) Lettings by resident landlords

A letting by a landlord of part of his own home is also specifically excluded from being an assured tenancy, and is probably the most common form of letting. So long as the landlord has been and still is genuinely resident in the property at all times since the start of the tenancy there should be few problems. This type of letting is dealt with in more detail in Chapter 6. Where the tenant or licensee shares part of the accommodation with the landlord or his family, then he will also be classified as an excluded occupier and the landlord may well be able to regain possession without resorting to formal notices and an application to the court.

If none of these types of lettings is appropriate then a landlord who wishes to be sure of recovering his property has a choice between letting on a shorthold tenancy, or under an assured tenancy to which one of the Grounds in Part I of Schedule 2 to the Act applies. These types of letting are set out below and should be considered after Chapter 1 has been read so that the effect of the letting can be properly understood.

2. Assured shorthold tenancies

An assured shorthold tenancy, or "shorthold" as it will be referred to here, is a type of assured tenancy which allows a landlord to let his property for a fixed period of not less than six months. At the end of the term he can bring the tenancy to an end and recover possession provided the proper notices and formalities are complied with.

Like any other fixed term tenancy, the landlord can obtain possession before the end of the term on Grounds 2, 8 or 10 to 15 in

Schedule 2 of the Act if there is provision in the tenancy agreement to terminate on those Grounds. Examples of these Grounds include where the tenant has broken one of the obligations of the tenancy such as the obligation to pay rent; and, if the property is mortgaged, where the lender wishes to sell it. Once the term has expired, a tenant who remains in possession, does so as a statutory periodic tenant until he leaves. If he does not leave voluntarily, he can remain until a court makes an order for possession.

An order for possession must be made provided that the court is satisfied on three points:

(a) that the tenancy was a shorthold and it has come to an end; and
(b) that no new assured tenancy has been granted to the tenant (whether shorthold or not); and
(c) that the landlord has given the tenant two months' notice that he requires possession of the property.

Before a property owner grants a shorthold tenancy he should check that such a tenancy suits his own requirements and also that the property is appropriate for a shorthold letting. The basic requirements for a shorthold tenancy are as follows:

(a) The letting must be for a fixed term and cannot be for less than six months. This means that the tenancy must run for six months from the day it is granted and not from some earlier date.
(b) The tenancy agreement must not allow the landlord to bring the tenancy to an end before the expiry of the six month period except where the tenant is actually in breach of the agreement.
(c) The landlord cannot grant a shorthold tenancy to an existing assured or Rent Act tenant in an attempt to weaken the existing tenant's position. If the tenant is already in occupation under an assured tenancy the new tenancy will not be binding on the tenant and he will simply continue as an assured tenant.
(d) The landlord should not be resident on the premises.
(e) The landlord *must* give the tenant notice in the form laid down by the Act so that the tenant knows his rights. It is essential that this notice is served by the landlord on the tenant before the tenancy is entered into and it *must* state that the tenancy which is to be granted will be an assured shorthold tenancy.

In order to appreciate the nature of a shorthold letting, the points listed above are now discussed more fully.

(a) The term of the tenancy

If a property owner wishes to grant a shorthold tenancy the Act requires that it should be a fixed term tenancy for a "term certain" of not less than six months. For a landlord to be sure that he has granted a term certain he would be advised to fix an initial period of at least six months which cannot be terminated by him unless there is a breach by the tenant of any obligation of the tenancy. Most tenancy agreements contain clauses called *forfeiture clauses* which allow the landlord to regain possession of his property if the tenant fails to pay the rent or perform his part of the agreement. These clauses should be included in a shorthold tenancy agreement. Once the initial six month period has ended, if the landlord wishes to grant a further tenancy, he has a choice of three courses of action:

(a) A new agreement can be made for a fixed term in the same terms as the old agreement.

(b) A memorandum can be written on the existing agreement recording that the tenancy is continuing for a further fixed period and that either the terms will remain the same, or that the parties have agreed to vary them. This must be signed and dated by both parties and could be worded as follows:

"We understand that if the tenant remains in occupation the tenancy will continue on the terms contained in this agreement unless expressly varied as set out below."

Any agreed variations, such as that the agreement can be terminated by either party giving the other two months' notice, can then be set out. It is also common to vary the rent at this stage.

(c) The tenant may be allowed to remain in possession paying rent at the same intervals as before and becomes a periodic tenant.

Whichever option is chosen, the Act provides that the new tenancy will also be a shorthold so long as the landlord, the tenant and the premises remain the same. In effect, once a shorthold tenancy has been granted and the initial requirements have been complied with, all subsequent tenancies will also be shorthold tenancies. This will be the case even if on a subsequent tenancy the term is for less than six months and the landlord has not served the relevant notice. The only exception is where the landlord serves a notice on the tenant before the new tenancy commences stating that it will *not* be a shorthold tenancy.

(b) Existing assured tenants

A landlord who already has an assured tenant in his property cannot then grant him a shorthold tenancy in an attempt to remove his security of tenure. The Act provides that a tenancy granted in these circumstances cannot be a shorthold tenancy. The same would apply to a landlord with existing protected tenants under the Rent Act 1977, since any new tenancy granted to them could not be either an assured or a shorthold tenancy. A landlord who has a tenant with a shorthold tenancy granted before 15 January 1989 should consult page 30. Note that any new tenancy which is granted to an existing shorthold tenant after 15 January 1989 will automatically be an assured shorthold tenancy even if the landlord has not complied with all the formal requirements.

(c) Resident landlords

The granting of a shorthold tenancy is not appropriate where the landlord is resident on the premises and occupies them as his only or principal home. A tenancy granted by a resident landlord is not an assured tenancy and the tenant will not be entitled to security of tenure in any event. For further information on letting rooms in a landlord's home see Chapter 6.

(d) The requirement for formal notice

It is *essential* that the proper form of notice is given in *all* cases of shorthold tenancies, as failure to do so may well mean that the tenant cannot be evicted. The Act has four basic requirements:

(a) the notice must be served *before* the tenancy is entered into;
(b) it must be served by the person who will be the landlord under the tenancy (or his agent) on the person who will be the tenant;
(c) the notice must state that the tenancy to which it relates is to be an assured shorthold tenancy; and
(d) the notice must be in the prescribed form.

The prescribed form of the notice is laid down in regulations called The Assured Tenancies and Agricultural Occupancies (Forms) Regulations 1988. These set out exactly what must be stated in the notice and should be followed. The court does have a discretion to put right or ignore minor slips in the notice, but if possible these ought to be avoided. If no notice is given at all this will cause considerable difficulties. See Appendix 1, page 132, for the form of notice.

(e) Rent

The difference between a shorthold tenancy and an ordinary assured tenancy is that a shorthold tenant has no security of tenure but can seek a reduced rent in certain circumstances. In general the rent charged for an assured tenancy cannot be altered unless the parties agree, but there are occasions when an application may be made to a rent assessment committee to determine a rent and these were discussed in Chapter 1.

Briefly, a rent assessment committee can only fix the rent to be charged in three cases:

(a) where there is a statutory periodic tenancy and it is wished to alter the terms;
(b) in a periodic tenancy, where the landlord wants to increase the rent and at least a year has passed;
(c) in a shorthold tenancy where the tenant considers that the rent is too high.

In each case, before the committee can make a determination of the rent, the matter must be referred to it by one or both of the parties. Although all three cases may apply to shorthold tenancies the most important of these is the automatic right of the tenant to apply to a rent assessment committee. This right arises once the landlord has served the notice in prescribed form which makes the tenancy a shorthold. However, the tenant is not allowed to make such an application in two circumstances:

(a) where the rent for the tenancy has already been determined in accordance with this procedure; or
(b) where the tenancy is one which was granted by the landlord after the expiry of a previous shorthold tenancy and therefore no notice was necessary.

If the tenant makes the application it must be in the form prescribed and the committee will determine a rent which it thinks the landlord might reasonably be expected to obtain under the tenancy. The committee is not allowed to make any determination of the rent unless first satisfied that there is a sufficient number of similar properties in the area let on assured tenancies, and that the rent charged for the property in question is significantly higher than it should be in the light of the rent charged for these other tenancies.

Once the committee has determined the rent to be charged the new rent will take effect from whatever date the committee decides. The date will not be earlier than the date of the application, but once the determination has been made the landlord will not be able to recover any rent from the tenant which is in excess of the rent determined. As in any other determination, the rent fixed by the committee will not include rates.

The effect of this for the landlord is that he may agree a rent with the tenant for a fixed period, only to find that the tenant then applies to the rent assessment committee. Whatever rent the committee determines will become the maximum rent which can be charged for the property until the fixed period expires. The landlord is not allowed to serve any notice increasing the rent under the tenancy until a year after the date of the determination. If a notice of increase is then served the procedure for referring this notice to a rent assessment committee will be the same as for any other assured tenancy (see page 134).

In view of the powers of a rent assessment committee to fix the rent of a shorthold tenancy a landlord who wishes to let property on a shorthold should check the level of rents which have been determined by his local committee. The president of each committee has to make this information publicly available and anyone wishing to see it should contact the local council housing department.

(f) Recovery of possession at the end of the tenancy

If the landlord wishes to regain possession of the property at the end of the agreed term he must give the tenant at least two months' notice of his intention to bring the tenancy to an end. This notice can be given at any time by letter advising the tenant that he must vacate the property in two months' time or when the tenancy expires (whichever is the later), and that if he does not do so possession proceedings will be instituted.

So long as the landlord has given the minimum of two months' notice to the tenant before the end of the term of the tenancy the tenant will no longer have any right to remain in occupation when the term ends. If he does, then the landlord can bring possession proceedings as soon as the tenancy has come to an end. If the tenancy has already expired before the landlord has given notice he can still obtain possession provided that he gives the tenant adequate notice. A notice in these circumstances should give the tenant at least two months to vacate the property and should expire at the end of a period of the tenancy, that is, at the end of a week, a month or a quarter, as appropriate.

Where a tenant has been given adequate notice but has not left the property at the end of the tenancy a landlord must bring possession proceedings. In order to institute proceedings in the county court a landlord should either contact his local county court and bring proceedings himself, or he may consult a solicitor, who will prepare the necessary documents on his behalf.

Until the court makes its order, a tenant is entitled to remain in possession as a statutory periodic tenant and should continue to pay the rent on the same terms as before.

Where a shorthold tenant fails to pay rent, or is in serious breach of any of his obligations under the tenancy, a landlord can bring possession proceedings relying on one of the Grounds required by the Act before the fixed term expires. In this case a landlord must serve a notice of proceedings for possession, setting out the particulars of the Ground upon which he relies. Possession will be granted only if the tenancy agreement provides that the tenancy can be terminated on that Ground, and the landlord would be advised to seek the assistance of a solicitor who should first warn the tenant to put matters right before proceedings are instituted.

(g) Sub-letting

It is normal practice for a shorthold tenancy agreement to include a provision against a tenant sub-letting the whole or any part of the premises. If a tenant does sub-let, the rights of a sub-tenant will come to an end at the same time as the rights of the original tenant, in any event. Where there is a clause in the tenancy agreement against sub-letting, a landlord may be able to apply for an order for possession before the tenancy ends because of the breach of the clause.

(h) The use of shorthold tenancies

Shorthold tenancies are mainly of use where a landlord wants to be sure of regaining possession of his property but cannot rely on any of the special categories of letting provided by the Act. Because shorthold tenancies need be for a six month period only, they can be used for letting property in the short term while a landlord decides what to do with it. They are also useful for letting farm cottages which may be needed for the housing of agricultural workers at some time in the future, or for property which is intended to house employees or relatives.

The main disadvantage of these tenancies is the degree of control exercised over the rent charged. A landlord may find that the rent which he expected to receive from his property is drastically reduced, and until the practice of rent assessment committees has been established in relation to these tenancies it is difficult to know what will be considered to be a reasonable rent for a particular property.

It is recommended that if a shorthold tenancy is to be used the landlord makes sure that there is a proper agreement and that the correct notices have been given. Initially the tenancy should be for the minimum six month period, and then, if both parties are happy with the arrangement, the tenancy can be extended for another six months or longer. Since it may always take a landlord longer than expected to regain possession even when adequate notice has been given, it is clearly advisable that the tenant should be chosen with care. Choosing a tenant is dealt with in Chapter 3.

(i) Existing shorthold tenancies

If a shorthold tenancy was granted before 15 January 1989 it is known as a *protected* shorthold tenancy and is governed by the provisions of the Rent Act 1977 (as amended by the Housing Act 1980).

A landlord who wants to recover possession of property let to a protected shorthold tenant must give written notice advising the tenant that he has *three months* to vacate the premises and that if he does not, possession proceedings will be instituted within *three months* of the expiry of the notice.

The earliest that notice of recovery of possession can be given is three months before the end of the tenancy. The latest that it can be given is the day before the tenancy comes to an end. If notice is not given during that three month period, then a tenant is entitled to remain in possession on the same terms for another year, and a landlord cannot serve notice until three months before the end of that year.

Possession proceedings have to be brought in the county court within three months of the expiry of the notice.

If a protected shorthold tenant breaks any of his obligations under the tenancy, for example if he fails to pay the rent, the landlord can apply to the court for an order for possession before the tenancy ends.

Protected shorthold tenancies are subject to rent control and a tenant can apply to a rent officer to have a fair rent registered; the fair rent may be well below the market rent.

Where a landlord has an existing protected shorthold tenant and grants him a new tenancy after 15 January 1989, the new tenancy will be an *assured* shorthold tenancy, even though the landlord has not given the necessary notices under the Housing Act 1988. This will be the case whether the old tenancy came to an end before or after 15 January 1989 so long as no other tenancy was granted in the meantime.

---

3. Other lettings where possession must be ordered

If a landlord does not wish to let on shorthold but still wants to be sure of recovering possession of his property, he has the alternative of letting under one of the Grounds where the Act provides that possession *must* be ordered. These Grounds are set out in Part I of Schedule 2 to the Act. While there are eight Grounds in this part of the Act, only two of them are really relevant to most landlords. Under Ground 1, owner-occupiers can let property which they may want to re-occupy at some time; and under Ground 3 the owners of holiday cottages can let their properties out of season. Both Grounds require special notices to be served on the tenant at the beginning of the tenancy.

(a) Owner-occupiers

Owner-occupiers in many different circumstances may wish to let their home – for example, owners of property which has been bought for retirement purposes; people who have to work abroad; servicemen; or those who have tied accommodation such as clergymen or school masters.

The Act does not deal with any of these categories specifically but provides a general Ground where possession can be recovered by owner-occupiers at the end of the tenancy. Ground 1 covers two different types of situation. Possession must be granted if *either*:

    (a) at some time before the tenancy was granted the landlord, or one of the landlords if the property is jointly owned, occupied the property as his only or principal home; or

(b) the landlord or one of joint landlords requires the property as an only or principal home for himself or his spouse and he did not acquire his interest in the property by purchasing the freehold with the tenant already in possession.

In both cases the landlord *must* give written notice to the tenant at the commencement of the tenancy that possession might be recovered on this Ground. This is usually incorporated into the tenancy agreement and a form of notice and tenancy agreement is found in Appendix 1. If the appropriate notice has not been given then the court has a discretion to dispense with the notice requirement if it thinks it is just to do so.

From a practical viewpoint, so long as a landlord has either lived in a property himself or wishes to do so at some time in the future, he will be able to recover possession under Ground 1 provided he has given the necessary notice. What is not apparently covered by this Ground is the situation where the property may be needed at some future time for a member of a landlord's family other than a spouse. For example, a flat may be bought as an investment with the idea that at some time one of the landlord's children may want to live in it. Unless the landlord himself has actually occupied the flat as his only or main home before letting, or the property is both owned and let by the children (assuming they are over eighteen), it is wiser to let by shorthold.

The tenancy itself may be either for a fixed term or on a periodic basis. If it is for a fixed term the landlord must always bear in mind that he will not be able to get possession until the end of the fixed term unless the tenant breaks the tenancy agreement. In both cases, if the landlord wishes to regain possession he must serve a notice in prescribed form on the tenant telling him that he intends to begin possession proceedings on Ground 1. The tenant has to be given a minimum of two months' notice and, if the tenant still refuses to leave, court proceedings must be begun within twelve months of serving the notice.

(b) Letting of holiday properties out of season

Provided that a property owner has let his property for genuine holiday purposes at any time during a previous twelve month period, he may let the property for non-holiday purposes for a fixed period of up to eight months and recover possession at the end of the agreed term under Ground 3 of Schedule 2 to the Act.

Before a property owner enters into any such agreement he must give the tenant a notice to say that at some time within the previous twelve months, ending on the date of the commencement of the letting, the property was occupied for holiday purposes and that possession will be required at the end of the agreed term for holiday purposes. The tenancy agreement should incorporate the appropriate notice, and the effect of the agreement is not only to give the tenant proper notice under Ground 3, but also to define the terms under which the tenant occupies the property.

To summarise out-of-season lettings, the most important points to consider are as follows:

(a) The property must have been let for holiday purposes within a twelve month period before the date of commencement of the tenancy agreement.

(b) The tenancy agreement must be for a fixed period of no more than eight months. The owner should be advised to leave the property vacant for at least two weeks before the first holiday so that the property can be refurbished before commencement of the new holiday letting season.

(c) A tenant *must* be given notice that possession may be recovered under Ground 3 of Schedule 2 to the Housing Act 1988, and preferably the notice should be incorporated into the agreement. If the notice is not given on or before the beginning of the tenancy the landlord may have extreme difficulty in evicting the tenant at the end of the agreed term because the court has no discretion to dispense with the notice requirement.

(d) If a tenant does not leave the property at the end of the agreed period it will *always* be necessary to serve a notice seeking possession, then apply to the court for an order for possession if the tenant is still in occupation.

3

Arranging a letting

1. Preparing the property

Before starting to look for a tenant, it is important that the property is suitably equipped and as easy as possible to manage and maintain. There is little worse than having a dissatisfied tenant who is continually complaining of faults, either in the property itself or in the appliances. The outside and structure of the property are the landlord's responsibility and should be thoroughly checked and, if necessary, repaired before a tenancy commences. A landlord granting a lease for less than seven years cannot make external repairs the responsibility of the tenant (see page 18).

The interior decoration and appliances should also be of a reasonable standard. If the property has no signs of damp and the decoration is in good order, the tenant is more likely to treat the property with care. In the case of furnished lettings, the furniture and equipment should be of a reasonable quality and in keeping with the type and state of the property. If the property is being let furnished, there should be sufficient crockery, cutlery, cooking utensils and other essential items; they should be both durable and of reasonable quality. There should be blankets or duvets, and two pillows, for each bed, but tenants are usually expected to bring their own linen. The beds should have washable calico covers, and each bedroom should have a wardrobe. It is not usual to provide a T.V. as a tenant should either provide one himself or arrange his own rental. It is always expected that a T.V. aerial is installed.

If it is felt the property is suitable for students, then clearly the accommodation and furniture need not be luxurious, but should be basic, durable and clean.

Some people will take partly furnished properties, which usually have carpets and curtains to an appropriate standard, together with kitchen appliances, which should also be suitable and appropriate to the type and condition of property being let. If the property is a flat, maisonette or a mews house with adjoining occupiers, there may be covenants restricting the occupiers to a single person or family and no shared occupancy. If there is any doubt this should be checked from the deeds, because if there is a breach of covenant the landlord may face a claim from the tenant as well as from the person who is able to enforce the covenant.

If the property is in a good residential area with a demand for high class accommodation, it may be advisable to upgrade it to a tasteful and luxurious standard. Very high rents may well be achieved from companies and overseas visitors who are often attracted to such accommodation. To find out more about specialist lettings and local demand, try contacting a local managing agent, show him the property and listen to his views.

Before making a decision, ensure as far as possible that you have considered the alternatives carefully and the type of letting you have chosen is the most suitable for you and your property.

2. Letting a mortgaged property

If the property is mortgaged then it is always essential that written permission for the letting is obtained from the building society or bank which granted the mortgage. They will have a standard form of notice which will have to be signed by both the landlord and the prospective tenant. It is common practice for the building society or bank to impose a penalty of between 1% and 2% over the existing mortgage rate, as the potential letting is regarded as a commercial arrangement. A landlord should also remember that once the property is let he may lose the benefit of tax relief on the mortgage (see page 89).

If an individual wishes to purchase a property for letting as an investment, and borrow the money from a bank to do so, a bank will usually expect the borrower to find at least 50% of the purchase price, the bank providing the balance. Their security will be a first legal mortgage over the property, and sometimes they request a second charge over another property. If a loan can be agreed, there is usually an arrangement fee, but this is negotiable. The rate of interest charged is usually 2½%–3% over the bank base rate.

It is also advisable, when letting a mortgaged property, to give the tenant a notice under Ground 2 that possession of the property may be recovered (see page 10). If this notice is not given and the lender (bank or building society) later wishes to sell – usually because the borrower has defaulted on the repayments – it may have to do so with a sitting tenant and the property will be worth much less.

---

3. Finding potential tenants

There are two aspects to selecting the person(s) to whom the property should be let, first, locating potential tenants; and second, identifying those most likely to prove suitable in terms of leaving the property at the end of the tenancy; ability to afford the rent; and the likelihood that the property and furniture will be respected. The reasons for choosing with care are clear. No landlord or prospective landlord wishes to be burdened with the inconvenience and probable expense of court proceedings to evict an unscrupulous tenant. Even if the tenant is fair and trustworthy and wishes to leave the property at the end of the agreed term, he may have nowhere to go. Although the local authority has a statutory duty to rehouse an unintentionally homeless person, it may well decline to do so until a court order has been made, so the landlord will still have to apply to the court for an order for possession.

The approach taken by a landlord in finding a tenant depends not only on the circumstances of the landlord and the type of property he proposes to let, but also on the locality of the property and the types of tenant looking for accommodation in that area. Some methods of finding potential tenants are set out below.

(a) Advertising

An advertisement may be placed in the local newspaper or local advertising magazine. If the local council has an accommodation register at the Information Centre, then steps should be taken to include the property in this list. The number of responses to an advertisement clearly depends on the area, but is often large as there is a general shortage of rented accommodation.

If possible, the advertisement should give a telephone number for enquirers to ring. When dealing with the calls, the owner should find out a little more about prospective tenants than their names, addresses and telephone numbers. It is advisable to make a list of questions in advance. These might include:

- whether or not the person is working;
- the reason for moving;
- how many people it is proposed should live in the property;
- whether or not there are any children or pets;
- the period for which the person proposes to rent the property; and
- where they propose to live when the tenancy expires.

The general manner and courtesy of the caller are also worthy of note. It is wise to make some notes when speaking to each enquirer. The next step is to select two or three of the most likely candidates, and arrange to meet them at the property. It is almost always a waste of time to meet every applicant; the most suitable ones should be identifiable from their telephone calls. The Housing Act will enable a landlord to charge agreed rents, but ensure as far as you are able that the tenant has the ability to pay what has been agreed.

(b) Local employers

If there is a particularly large company within, say, ten miles of the property, then the personnel officer may well be looking for temporary accommodation for employees. It is now becoming commonplace for companies to move their employees from one area to another which necessitates their moving house or working in another area for a short period. As noted earlier (see page 7), it is preferable if the company itself becomes the tenant because the Housing Act 1988 states that a company cannot have the benefit of security of tenure like an ordinary person. Letting to a company is dealt with in Chapter 2.

There is also the local city or town council, whose employees are often on the move, and there may well be some employees looking for temporary accommodation.

(c) Students

If the property is near a university, polytechnic or large college, or even within a twenty mile radius if there is a shortage of accommodation for students, it may be worth contacting the accommodation officer to see if the college might wish to rent the property for its students. If the letting cannot be undertaken through the college itself, then care must be taken in preparing a suitable tenancy agreement. Letting to students usually suggests that there will be one student for each bedroom and they will share the rest of the accommodation. The accommodation officer at the college should provide general assistance and advice on the rents to be charged, as well as advising on the suitability of the accommodation. Letting to students should be undertaken with some care; if a student cannot afford the market rent and runs up arrears it may well be that a landlord will have difficulty in recovering the rent due, as well as his legal fees if he has to bring possession proceedings. It is often wiser, when letting to students, to let to one nominated individual who alone will be responsible for all the rent. The number of people with whom he can share must also be made clear in a tenancy agreement.

(d) Recommendation

A safer means of finding a tenant is by recommendation. This does not mean that care need not be taken in accepting a tenant recommended by a friend or acquaintance – indeed, if the tenant does prove to be unreliable or untrustworthy, it may lead to some embarrassment!

(e) Agents

An easier way may well be to instruct a managing agent to find a tenant and carry out the necessary administration in connection with the letting. The aspects involved in using a managing agent are dealt with more fully below (see page 39).

4. Selecting a tenant

When interviewing applicants, the landlord should keep in mind that the better the tenant, the more likely it is that the landlord will profit from the letting. It helps to be a good intuitive judge of character when considering applicants; even if you are not, some fairly searching questions, going over all the points listed on page 37, will be revealing. An interesting and often accurate pointer of how a prospective tenant may look after a property is how presentable they are, and how their car is kept.

References should be requested and taken up, unless there is some special and compelling reason not to do so. It is usual to ask for three referees and these should be an employer; someone known to the tenant for at least two years who is not a relative; and a bank. It is usual practice when seeking a bank reference to obtain the reference "bank to bank", that is, the landlord's bank contacts the referee bank direct. On requesting references it is advisable to state that the reply will be treated in strict confidence.

Although the Housing Act 1988 introduces market rents, which will be very much higher than the old so-called "fair" rents the new regime will bring with it its own problems. In particular, the landlord must now seriously consider the ability of the tenant to pay. The DSS will not necessarily pay an excessive rent even though it may have been agreed between the landlord and the tenant claimant. This is another indicator of the care that needs to be taken when considering prospective tenants.

5. Accommodation agencies and managing agents

(a) The pro's and con's

It is now common for a landlord to let his property through either an accommodation agency, or a specialist management service which many estate agents and managing agents now offer. There are some firms who specialise in *residential* management, and they let mainly to companies which are able to pay the higher rents. The hazards and advantages of letting to a company are explained in Chapter 2 (see pages 21 to 23) and should be considered carefully.

The benefit of using an agency is that it takes the administration work away from the landlord and the agent can be left to find a tenant, take up references, and advise on rental and the best method of letting the property. He should assist in finding tenants to meet the landlord's requirements, and prepare and complete a tenancy agreement. A managing agent often charges a considerable amount for finding a tenant before even starting any management. This is dealt with later, but a good specialist agency can often justify its charges by finding a good tenant paying a high rent.

The agent can be commissioned to handle all aspects of the letting, including handing over the keys, collecting the rent and keeping an eye on the property. A good managing agent will make a regular inspection and report back to the landlord to confirm that the condition of the property is being maintained. It is also helpful for a managing agent to deal with any complaints which crop up; these may relate to the property, appliances or even to troublesome neighbours. A well-established agency should have considerable experience in all aspects of property management and should therefore be well able to deal with problems as they arise.

(b) Mortgaged property

The managing agent will want to know whether the property is mortgaged or not, and if it is, it is usually stipulated in the mortgage deed that permission to let must be obtained from the building society or bank. A copy of the consent should be given to the agents to ensure that any special terms are complied with, and that the agent is acquainted with any conditions imposed by the mortgage. If there is any doubt then the landlord should pass on the form of notice received from his mortgagees to the managing agents who will deal with the building society or bank direct. A good managing agent should obtain legal advice where necessary, but if there is a problem over the consent it is advisable to consult a solicitor.

(c) Service accounts

As far as the general and water rates are concerned, the landlord should let the managing agents know how much these are, as they should be included in the rent. If the property is a flat, then there should also be included the ground rent and the likely maintenance charges. Some accounts, such as telephone, gas and electricity, should be transferred into the tenant's name from the date of commencement of the tenancy. In letting a furnished or even part furnished property, the domestic equipment provided for the tenant's use should be in good working order. Some agents prefer landlords to take out service contracts for equipment such as washing machines, dishwashing machines, cooking appliances and central heating systems, so that if there is any serious fault it will be attended to immediately. It is advisable to ensure that the central heating system is serviced regularly.

(d) Income tax and the managing agent

Taxation is dealt with in full in Chapter 7, but it is worth noting here that where a landlord's normal place of abode is overseas, the Inland Revenue may call upon the collecting agent to deduct tax at the standard rate on the profit element of the rent. Most agents pay over the rent to such landlords in the usual way, but keep back as a reserve the equivalent of the amount of tax payable at the basic rate. An agent should keep his client informed at monthly intervals of the amounts collected and tax deducted.

A landlord living overseas may nominate a person (such as an accountant) to act as his agent for collection and for computation and payment of tax due. In this case the payments will be paid gross to the accountant after deduction of the agent's own expenses. The Revenue will normally raise a provisional assessment in October in respect of the year ending the following April. If the assessments are sent to the managing agent, they should immediately be forwarded to the landlord's accountant so that, if appropriate, an appeal may be lodged and the proper returns completed. It should be noted that the Revenue can charge interest on late payments of tax from the date of an appeal, so it is advisable for the assessments to be dealt with promptly.

(e) Tenancy agreements prepared by an agent

It is usual for managing agents to prepare a tenancy agreement at a fee in the region of £20 to £30. The agreement and any notices given to the tenant must be signed by the owners of the property, who must sign in the presence of an independent witness who should add his or her name, address and occupation. If the property is leasehold, a copy of the covenants affecting the property should be given to the managing agents so that these may be included in the tenancy agreement.

It is also necessary to include in the agreement an inventory of the contents. If this is prepared by the managing agents, the basic charge for preparing it may be in the region of £10 to £15 per room. On vacating the premises, the managing agent will be expected to check that the items listed in the inventory are present and that the property is given up in a condition similar to that when the letting began. In some cases it is necessary for a schedule of condition to be prepared, detailing the state of the property and listing any faults or damage to the property itself, or to the decoration and furniture. If any damage has been done by the tenant (apart from fair wear and tear), then a sum will be deducted from the deposit given at the outset. It is advisable to prepare a schedule of condition to reduce the possibility of a dispute when a tenancy expires. A deposit is usually equivalent to at least one month's rent and is held by the managing agents in their client account.

(f) Fees

Most managing agents will charge a fee based on a percentage of the rent. The percentage varies depending on the amount of administration expected of the managing agents. Instructing an agent on a full management basis, which would include finding a tenant; collecting rent; attending to the tenant's complaints; paying accounts; dealing with repairs and carrying out inspections, may justify a charge of 15%. For finding a tenant only, then the charge may, in London, be as high as 10% of the annual rent, or as low as one week's rent in the provinces. These expenses are of course deductable against income for tax purposes.

Although their fees may appear high, it may well be that an agent who has a large number of enquiries may find a suitable tenant who pays more than a landlord would otherwise obtain, even allowing for the agent's commission. A managing agent, like a tenant, should be selected with care.

6. The tenancy agreement

Once the type of letting has been decided and a suitable tenant has been found, then it is necessary to prepare a tenancy agreement. Some draft agreements can be seen in Appendix 1 (see pages 108 to 117), but these are for guidance only; more clauses may need to be added and some deleted. The agreement must obviously be tailored to suit the requirements of each particular case, and it is always wise to consult a solicitor for advice and to draft a tenancy agreement.

If certain proper formalities are not complied with at the beginning of the tenancy, it may be that a landlord loses his right to get his property back, even when the term of the tenancy expires. The kinds of tenancy, and the advantages and disadvantages of each, are discussed in Chapters 1 and 2. To recap, there are three main types:

(a) A shorthold tenancy under the Housing Act 1988, where possession at the end is fairly certain, but strict formalities must be complied with.

(b) A letting under one of the Grounds where a tenant must vacate when required. These are *Ground 1* where a property is let by an owner/occupier, or *Ground 3* for a short letting after a holiday let. Both of these are discussed in Chapter 2 and the rules relating to each of them must be noted carefully. The common feature of these two Grounds is that the tenant should, on or before commencement of a tenancy, receive a notice to say that the landlord will wish to recover possession of the property under the particular Ground at the end of the period of the tenancy. If the property is mortgaged it is advisable also to give the tenant notice under Ground 2 that the property may be recovered under that Ground.

(c) An assured tenancy, which enables the landlord to recover the agreed rent but the tenant does have security of tenure, that is, he will become a sitting tenant and so long as the rent is paid and he complies with the terms of the tenancy he can stay indefinitely.

For shorthold tenancies a different form of agreement has to be used, and a special notice must be given in addition to the agreement itself. It is a strict condition that the tenant must be given this notice *before* the tenancy commences. The notice states his rights as far as the tenancy is concerned.

Having decided which type of tenancy is the most suitable, the landlord can himself prepare a suitable agreement, as long as he fully understands the legal implications of the tenancy he is granting, and can ensure that all the essential clauses and notices are included in the agreement. It is, though, strongly advised to seek professional advice on the preparation of a tenancy agreement.

The steps for preparing and entering into an agreement are briefly, as follows:

(a) Having identified the type of tenancy most suitable, an appropriate model agreement (see, for example, Appendix 1, pages 108 to 117) should be selected.

(b) Any required notice which relates to the proposed letting should be incorporated into the agreement or given to the prospective tenant before the agreement is entered into.

(c) Care should be taken to ensure that the agreement provides for rights of entry and inspection on reasonable notice, and for termination of the tenancy for breach of the tenant's obligations.

(d) The agreement should then be typed. If there is likely to be more than one letting, it is helpful to have the agreement typed leaving blanks for the names and addresses of the parties, the term, and the rent. Several copies can then be taken at the same time. If it is inconvenient to use and prepare an agreement from one of the specimen agreements given in this book, then a pre-printed agreement can be purchased from a firm of law stationers (see the *Yellow Pages*).

(e) A room by room inventory should be compiled and annexed to the agreement ready for signature by both parties. Any damage to the furniture or equipment should be noted in the inventory.

(f) A schedule of condition should be prepared, showing the condition of the interior of the property, including the state of decoration and furnishings, and any damage that is already present.

(g) Once all the terms have been agreed, the blanks may be filled in with the tenant present. The landlord signs one copy of the agreement, the inventory and the schedule of condition; and the tenant signs a second copy of the three documents. The date is written onto all the documents, and the parties then exchange the signed papers so that the tenant has the copies which the landlord signed, and vice versa.

(h) Upon exchange of agreements the landlord should receive the first month's rent, and a returnable breakage/damage deposit equivalent to, say, one month's rent. A receipt should be given to the tenant indicating that the deposit is held in respect of any damage to or loss of the landlord's property, furnishings, equipment or state of decoration. Upon full payment, the keys can be handed to the tenant.

Note that it is illegal to accept a premium, that is, a sum of money paid by a prospective tenant simply to be granted a tenancy.

7. Stamp duty

A lease or tenancy agreement must in some circumstances be stamped by any of the Stamp Offices mentioned below. The rate of duty differs depending on the term of the tenancy, the rent charged and whether or not the property is furnished. After the documents have been completed and exchanged, the landlord should attend to the stamping.

There are a few concessions exempting stamp duty altogether from certain short term tenancies, or reducing it to a nominal amount. These are, briefly, as follows:

(a) In the case of a furnished tenancy of a dwelling-house for a fixed term of less than a year where the rent does not exceed £500 per year, there is no duty payable.

(b) If the rent of a dwelling-house exceeds £500 and the period of the tenancy is less than a year, the duty is a nominal £1.

(c) On any tenancy agreement of any other property where there is a fixed term of less than seven years or the term is periodic, and the rent does not exceed £500 per year, there is no duty at all.

For any other lease or tenancy agreement where the term does not exceed seven years, stamp duty must be paid. The rate for tenancies, where the annual rent exceeds £500, is 50p for every £50, or part of £50, of the rent.

The copy of the agreement signed by the landlord has to be stamped as described above; the part signed by the tenant (the counterpart) is stamped with a nominal 50p stamp only.

The addresses of the main Stamp Offices are:

Birmingham	Edmund House, 12–22 Newhall Street, Birmingham B3 3DU
Bristol	First Floor, The Pithay, All Saints Street, Bristol BS1 2NY
Cardiff	Companies House, Crown Way, Cardiff CF4 3UR
Leeds	42 Eastgate, Leeds LS2 7LD
Liverpool	Tower Buildings, Water Street, Liverpool L3 1AE
London	South-West Wing, Bush House, Strand, WC2B 4QN
Manchester	Albert Bridge House, Bridge Street, Manchester M60 9BT
Newcastle-upon-Tyne	Room 222, Aidan House, All Saints Office Centre, Newcastle-upon-Tyne, NE1 5NN
Nottingham	Lambert House, Talbot Street, Nottingham NG1 5NN
Worthing	West Block, Barrington Road, Worthing, BN12 4SF

The agreements should be sent, with a cheque or postal order made payable to "Inland Revenue", addressed to the Office of the Controller of Stamps at the appropriate office. The absence of a proper stamp does not render the document invalid, but if it is not stamped it may not be produced in court and used in evidence, for example, in possession proceedings should they become necessary. If there is any doubt, the Stamp Office can advise.

Holiday lettings

A letting strictly for holiday purposes does not give the tenant any right to remain in occupation after the agreed period has expired. It is essential that the true purpose of the letting is a holiday, and that the arrangement is not simply a device to ensure repossession. It is, however, possible for a holiday letting to be of several months' duration, as long as the true purpose is a holiday.

There are useful provisions to enable a property owner to let his property after the last holiday let for a continuous period of up to eight months. These out-of-season lets do not give the tenant any protection to stay in the property after the tenancy has expired, *provided certain notices are given*. The formalities required were dealt with in Chapter 2 (see page 33). Using this form of tenancy, the property is occupied during the out-of-season months and the landlord can be sure of recovering possession at the end of the letting. If the tenant does not then go peacefully, a court order is required.

Many factors have to be taken into account to establish whether a property and its location make it suitable for holiday letting. For the owner considering letting a property for holidays, there are also other matters to be kept in mind, such as having someone available to keep an eye on the property during the letting periods, to show people in and out and to arrange or undertake cleaning after each letting. There must also be someone willing to undertake the administration – organising the lettings, advertising, taking bookings, writing letters and so on. The purpose of this chapter is to give the reader some background to help decide whether a property is suitable for holiday lettings; and to provide some guidelines in setting up and organising holiday lettings generally.

For the purposes of holiday letting, the property must itself be suitable, in immediate surroundings acceptable to prospective visitors, and in an area that is generally regarded as being appropriate for such letting.

Firstly, regarding the property itself, it should be appreciated that a higher standard is generally required for holiday letting. The property must be maintained in good decorative condition, comfortably furnished and well-carpeted: the higher the general standard of the property, the higher the rent – and the fewer the complaints.

Regarding the immediate location of a property, it would not be suitable for holiday letting if it is near an opencast coal mine, for example, or cooling towers, or even has noisy neighbours. The prospective visitor is quite rightly a discerning person who will always be critical if anything affects the enjoyment of his holiday.

If the property and its immediate location are suitable, it will still have to be in an area that is attractive to holidaymakers. If advice is required to establish whether there is a local need, contact the regional tourist board for guidance.

The English Tourist Board and the Welsh Tourist Board have, with the support and co-operation of respective Regional Tourist Boards, introduced a Holiday Homes Approval Scheme. As part of their object to promote tourism in their area, this scheme not only sets a minimum standard for self-catering holiday homes, but also offers a wealth of useful and invaluable advice. This includes guidance as to whether property is suitable for holiday letting. Advice on marketing is also offered. In fact, the scheme is generally found to be extremely helpful and constructive on any aspect of holiday letting. As each property needs to be considered for holiday letting on its own merits any potential landlord should contact the regional tourist board for subjective guidance, clear advice and, if necessary, some encouragement.

The Holiday Homes Approval Scheme has been designed to identify and acknowledge those self-catering holiday homes that have been inspected and found to conform to the Tourist Board minimum standards for approval and to the Tourist Board's Code of Conduct. If a holiday home does conform, the property may be promoted as "English (or Welsh) Tourist Board Approved".

The main conditions which must be satisfied for participation in the Holiday Homes Approval Scheme are:

(i) If the establishment consists of two or more holiday home units, all the units must meet the minimum requirements for approval.
(ii) All "Approved" establishments must:
  • observe the "Code of Conduct" (see below);
  • be inspected annually;
  • pay an annual participation fee;
  • complete periodic information questionnaires.
(iii) If an "Approved" establishment acquires additional units, these must be included in the scheme.
(iv) Units that are sold as "Approved" may not be promoted as such until re-inspection.
(v) Failure to observe the conditions may result in the establishment being ineligible to display the Tourist Board's "Approval" badge or other endorsement.

The scheme lays down minimum standards and detailed requirements in a booklet for holiday home owners. This lists basic requirements regarding accommodation, including specific minimum standards for rooms, fittings and décor, plus a recommended inventory of equipment that should be provided. There is further included a Code of Conduct to which holiday home owners should conform, and similarly another Code of Conduct to be observed by agencies. These provide a fair and sensible framework in which to operate the letting of holiday homes.

1. Preparations

The property should be prepared for letting by equipping it with furniture and other items appropriate for the type of holiday makers to whom it will be let.

Furniture should be solid, comfortable and easily maintained and cleaned. It should be in keeping with the property; for example, if it is proposed to offer luxury holiday accommodation at a very high price, then clearly the furniture should similarly be of a high standard. There should also be included items to add to the character of the property, and to make it comfortable. A few pictures on the walls, the odd book, magazines, cards and even games are appreciated. Small or fragile items should usually be avoided because of the risk of breakages and/or pilferage.

The local Tourist Information Centre should be able to provide a few booklets outlining places of interest. Although you may have to pay for them, visitors will find them helpful. Visitors also often appreciate a sketch of the immediate vicinity, showing points such as bus stops, stations, the doctor's surgery, the chemist, restaurants, and sports facilities. Some owners put a map of the area on the wall and mark places of interest. All these will assist visitors in planning an enjoyable holiday, and will encourage return visits and recommendations.

Some specific items are worthy of consideration:

Linen – Some owners choose to provide linen, but it may be more trouble than it is worth, and it is not unreasonable to expect visitors based in the U.K. to bring their own. If you have visitors from overseas, linen should be provided and visitors should be told in advance of any extra charge. It is also wise to keep a spare set of linen in case of any unexpected need. Quilts may be preferred to blankets, but this is a matter of personal choice. Ease of cleaning or laundering are obvious points to keep in mind. It is advisable but by no means essential to have a cot available.

Pets – Many owners expressly forbid pets. Others, who allow pets, seldom have a problem. It is a matter of personal choice and much depends on the property itself, its location and furnishings, and whether the person responsible for cleaning is prepared to clean up after dogs and cats. Some owners specify that they take dogs by prior arrangement only or that they will allow only small dogs. If pets are allowed, the landlord should make clear that they must be kept under control at all times, and the animal's blanket or basket should be brought and used. It is now becoming common for owners to make an additional charge for a dog. Rates start at about £5 per week – considerably less than kennel charges.

Children – Some owners do not encourage young children, but again this is an individual matter, depending on the type and size of property, the furnishings and whether there are any items, such as antiques, which are more likely to be damaged by children. However, if children are prohibited altogether, or if a minimum age is set, then of course the opportunity of letting to many families with children is lost. These families do make up a large part of the potential market and attracting bookings is difficult enough.

Groceries – Some owners may be prepared to stock the kitchen with groceries specially ordered in advance by incoming visitors. As the self-catering holiday industry is becoming increasingly competitive this is now recommended. A service of this kind can help attract bookings, and can be offered at different levels. For example a standard pack of basic provisions can be provided and included in the price, or offered as an "extra" and charged.

Gas/electricity – In addition to the rent, visitors should pay for the gas and electricity which they use whilst in occupation. The easiest way to charge is to put in a coin meter, which is relatively cheap to buy, and can be installed by an electrician or gas fitter. The meter should be set so that the holiday maker is not paying more for power than is the landlord, because the landlord is now obliged by law not to charge over certain limits on power that is re-sold by him. A coin meter is not recommended for better quality and more expensive properties. For these, include gas and electricity in the rental. However, some owners of more expensive properties might prefer to take a "before-and-after" reading of the ordinary meter and then charge at the going rate. If this option is preferred then all advertising literature should make clear that power is to be paid for in this way.

Telephone – A telephone in the property may well add to its attractions. There are now several neat, compact table-top payphones available from British Telecom. The sales office can be contacted through the operator. The connection charge for a small table-top payphone is over £25, and rentals start at around £35 per quarter – considerably more for a larger installation. The person who rents the system from British Telecom is charged in the normal way for all the calls as if they had been made from an ordinary telephone; it is his obligation to empty the cash box and he keeps the money it contains. The holiday maker is charged at a special unit rate, which is slightly higher than the rate paid by the owner. It is said that the difference between the two unit rates could cover the quarterly rental, but this may be so only if the telephone is heavily used. It should also be kept in mind that most of these payphones are capable of receiving incoming calls, allowing the caller to reverse the charges, and leaving the property owner to pay the bill. It may therefore be worth ensuring that the phone cannot take incoming calls.

Television – It is undoubtedly an advantage to have a television, which should be a colour set, in the property. For convenience, it is preferable to rent rather than buy. If the set does go wrong, the visitor can telephone the TV rental firm direct, who are obliged to repair the fault. There is the added advantage that the rental is a deductible expense for tax purposes.

There has been some uncertainty as to whether a TV licence is needed for a set in self-catering property. The position has now been clarified by the National TV Licence Records Office and is as follows. If an owner of a single property used for holiday letting has a television installed in that property then an appropriate television licence will be required. Where an owner has more than one property within the same curtilage then he should apply to the National TV Licence Records Office, Bristol BS98 ITL (tel: 0272 219267) for a special licence. This licence will cover up to fifteen television sets within the same curtilage, but a further licence will be required for every additional five sets or units in excess of fifteen. If an owner has four holiday homes in four different locations then four licences will of course, be required. For additional information it is advisable to contact the TV Licence Records Office.

Heating – Obviously heating is not particularly important during the summer months, but some provision should be made in case of the odd cold evening, which is not unusual even during our warmest months. Efficient portable electric heaters may be the most appropriate method. If the property has central heating or storage radiators, the system should be turned off before each letting. The visitor can, of course, turn it on if he chooses. Whatever type of heating is provided, the power consumed should be metered and charged for (see above, page 51).

Cleaning – It is important that the property is refurbished before the start of the season and some decoration is usually necessary. The property should also be thoroughly cleaned before each letting, and if a cleaner is employed, he or she should be dependable and thorough. Many visitors leave the property as clean as they found it, but some do not. The type of property and area in which it lies often influence the kind of visitor. If the property is inland, then the visitor may well be a little more discerning than the average visitor to the seaside. In some areas, there is a danger of the property being abused or even vandalised. If there may be such a danger, a sizeable deposit for breakages is appropriate; it is important when taking the deposit to explain the reason. If the owner lives a distance from the property, he or she should arrange to have some local, and trustworthy, person, to keep an eye on things, check the property when guests leave, and hand back the deposit, less any deduction(s).

Receiving guests – Someone, preferably the owner, but if not, the local caretaker, should be on hand, not only to welcome visitors when they arrive and hand over the keys, but to answer any questions or to be on hand in case of an emergency. The same person can also make sure the property is clean and tidy, that the fridge is cold and the hot water has been turned on ready for new guests. It is always appreciated if tea is laid out ready, and a few flowers make visitors feel even more welcome. Return visits should be encouraged, so personal service and a pleasant welcome should never be underestimated. Quality of service and accommodation will be long remembered; the price soon forgotten.

Safety – The property owner should protect his own interests and those of the visitors. Everything should be as safe as possible. In particular, all electrical wiring, installations and equipment should be in good order and conform to the appropriate regulations and approved standards. If in doubt, an electrical contractor will check. There should be no dangerous edges or traps, either inside or outside the property. Young children in particular should be considered when checking for hazards. If the property is near a road, there should be a fence or gate to prevent young children or animals running out. It is recommended by the English Tourist Board that a first aid kit is provided, and put in an accessible place in the kitchen.

Lastly, and most importantly, the owner should have a public liability insurance policy covering the property to be let, and the property and contents should be fully insured. The insurance company should be notified that the property is being used for holiday lettings.

2. Fixing the price

In the early stages, the rental charged should be influenced by what is required to make the business viable, as well as by what other people are charging. Journals and newspapers carrying advertisements for holiday accommodation in the area can be consulted but care should be taken to compare like with like. Look at the size and accommodation, situation, amenities, the general standard of furnishings and so on.

Charges obviously vary throughout the year, higher prices applying during the school summer holidays. The out-of-season months should be considered in the light of the possibility of one winter let (with proper management), or an assortment of sporadic holiday or weekend lets.

Try to avoid underpricing the property, as too low a price may suggest that there is something wrong with the property. A property in a pleasant, desirable location should attract a very high weekly income; but a high rental should be matched by a well-produced brochure and efficient administration.

When taking bookings, it may be necessary to be flexible on pricing; if there are unbooked weeks shortly before the start of the season, a price reduction in order to fill them is wise, as void weeks earn nothing.

3. Marketing the property

Marketing is crucial, so much so that success or failure of a holiday letting season is dependent upon it.

For the beginner to the self-catering market, a good agency is strongly recommended, since it is a fairly easy and efficient way of marketing the property while learning the ropes. If you are considering embarking on a major project – setting up a number of self-catering units – it is advisable to seek professional help while the project is still on the drawing board. Significant expense should be avoided until a good understanding of this difficult market has been acquired.

In any event, a good first step is to contact the local tourist board, who have specialist knowledge and are usually able to provide invaluable assistance. It is helpful also to contact one of the major letting agencies, who should provide guidance from their considerable experience. A larger agency may have an area representative who should, without charge or obligation, discuss the various steps to be taken and the likely rent that may be achieved.

Having made some initial inquiries, the owner should decide whether to employ an agency to take care of the lettings, or to do it himself. Both these options are considered in more detail below, but in either case, the marketing activities must be undertaken in a professional manner if the business is to succeed. The local tourist boards do, in some circumstances, offer grants to assist in setting up self-catering units, but in view of problems arising from poor marketing, they now make it a condition of the grant that the marketing is placed in the hands of a recognised letting agency for the first, and sometimes the second, year of operation.

The importance of marketing should never be underestimated – a first-class project may be doomed to failure by inferior marketing. A typical example is when owners spend hundreds of pounds on expensive advertising and, on obtaining some response, send out poor quality literature, only to be met with no further interest. It is expensive to elicit enquiries, so every effort should be made to convert enquiries into bookings. The property details should be well presented in an attractive brochure. Appendix 3 (see page 140) gives a model of a type of brochure which can be used to great effect.

The alternatives – of marketing with or without an agency – are considered next.

4. Agencies

Many agencies handle self-catering accommodation in the UK. The Sunday newspapers carry many advertisements. There are some good, well-organised agencies, and others that should be avoided. A book of this kind can do no more than give broad advice for guidance in choosing an agency. The English Tourist Board may assist, but always check several agencies before making a decision. The following questions should be asked in respect of each agency being considered:

- What is their reputation?
- How long have they been in business?
- What is their average number of weeks booked per property?
- Does the agency cater for property of the same type as yours?
- Has their local representative been courteous and helpful and advised on making the most of your property?

- Examine their literature and brochure. Are you impressed? Will they present your property as attractively as possible?
- What is the price structure?
- How many brochures are printed and distributed?
- Do they keep a mailing list and send out the brochure to people who have booked or enquired before?
- What deposit is required on a booking?
- Do they require final payment in advance from prospective visitors?
- When do you get paid?
- What periods of exclusive agency do they require?
- Do they have a strict quality control system?
- Are the holidays they are selling of good quality and good value?
- Where do they advertise?
- How do they calculate their price structure?
- What is your net weekly rent?
- How are their fees calculated?
- Are their staff positive and enthusiastic?
- Do they answer the telephones seven days a week?

Finally, it is worth asking a prospective agent outright to show how they will increase your income and cut your costs. All these points reinforce the importance of selecting a good agent.

Agents charge up to 20% of the rental for their services. At first sight this may seem a lot, but compared with the owner's costs if he was to manage the property himself – bearing in mind that those costs include telephone, postage, advertising, time and much more – the agency commission may well prove good value.

There are some agencies in other European countries interested in taking English properties onto their books. There are dozens to choose from, but the Dutch, Germans and Belgians are most attracted to self-catering holidays in the U.K. For general advice on overseas agencies the English Tourist Board centre in the country in question may be contacted for advice and introductions.

When doing so, it is worth asking how popular U.K. self-catering is at the time. An important factor is the value of sterling against the European currencies; if the £ is relatively expensive, then people will not be keen to spend their holiday in the U.K.

Outside Europe, the main countries where interest may be found are the U.S., Canada, South Africa, Australia and New Zealand. Agencies in the U.S. are particularly keen to take U.K. properties onto their books. It is worth bearing in mind that American, Australian and South African tourists do regard an ice box and a shower as essential features. The English Tourist Board can usually help if a property owner wishes to let to overseas visitors, and often keeps a good supply of information for all sorts of holidays in the U.K. for overseas enquirers. The Board may appreciate a number of brochures which they can distribute to overseas enquirers.

5. "Do-it-yourself" marketing

(a) Preparing a brochure

There is no doubt that a good, professionally produced brochure *will* attract more enquiries and bookings than otherwise. The simple model brochure in Appendix 3 can be prepared by most printers at fairly low cost, but large printing companies tend to charge more and should therefore usually be avoided. It may well be that the art and design work, as well as the printing, can be undertaken by the printer. Alternatively you can instruct an advertising agent, who will probably be imaginative and creative, but may be expensive. Ask for a quotation before instructing an advertising agency; be sure that they are able to produce what you require, and ask if they have experience in producing such promotional material.

Briefly, the brochure should contain the following information:

- A brief description of the area and location of the property, with a good drawing of the property, a toned picture, a two-colour print, or even a sepia print. It is wise to take a printer's advice. Remember that once the expensive design work is sorted out, it is relatively inexpensive to print the brochures.
- A description of the general facilities, such as heating, telephone, television, kitchen equipment, washing-machine, linen, cot and drying facilities.
- Information about which facilities are charged for as "extras" and

the actual costs; and how gas, electricity and telephone calls are to
be paid for.
- Details of booking periods (often Saturday to Saturday) and the
  arrangements for receiving visitors on their arrival and handing
  over the keys.
- Rental charges and deposit arrangements.
- The owner's name and address.
- A map of the region with reference to places of interest, such as
  National Trust properties, beaches, sailing, walks, golf courses,
  recreational facilities and any other attractions.
- Information detailing distances to the nearest shops, Post Office,
  and public transport.
- Car parking arrangements.
- A description of the garden, outlook and garden furniture is
  relevant, and any other features of the property that may be of
  interest to visitors.

A note of caution – do advertise accurately – if the property lies under
the end of the main runway at Heathrow Airport you should say so!

A local printer should be able to type-set and undertake the printing
to a good standard. It is necessary to see a proof before the brochure
goes to press, as there may be last minute alterations or additions.

(b) Advertising

Once a stock of brochures has been printed, how are they distributed as
cost effectively as possible to fully book the property? The answer is
advertising of one sort or another. There are no hard and fast rules
about this and no substitute for experience.

Choose the wording carefully so as to be both concise and
informative. A reference to the building's unusual character or
architecture – its exposed beams or the fact that it is a former
gamekeeper's cottage, for example – are worth inclusion. Consider the
benefits that a holiday in your property would confer. A sun balcony or
a secluded terrace could give your advertisement the edge over the
others. Do not be afraid to mention a modern well-equipped kitchen.
Also consider the general location: mountain views and tumbling
waterfalls can appeal enormously to city-dwellers looking for a change.
If your area is good for golf, fishing or pony-trekking, mention it in
your advertisement. Never mislead! Do not advertise "beach nearby" if

in fact the beach is fifteen miles away, or inaccessible, unsafe or otherwise unsuitable.

Much depends on the style and length of the advertisements in the magazines or newspapers, and this of course is often dictated by costs. But an example of a satisfactory advertisement might be:

Little Tidley, Somerset

Thatched cottage for 4/6 with large inglenook fireplace in sitting room. Original flagstone floors. On edge of pretty village with 16th century pub. Surrounded by fruit orchards with views of rolling hills. Lovely coastal footpath walks. Excellent golf and fishing within easy reach. Local vineyards, cider and cheese farms nearby.

It is important to choose your advertising media with care, and, obviously, to attempt to secure the highest number of bookings for the minimum cost. It is difficult to generalise, since much depends on the type of property and its location. In considering advertising generally, a property owner might ask the following questions:

• What type of person would be interested in the property and what journals or papers would that type of person consult when looking for a holiday home?
• How much should sensibly be spent on advertising, and has an allowance to cover this cost been put into the proposed rental charges?
• What kind of advertising is most appropriate; for example, a de luxe property may well justify the expense of advertising in the national press.

The regional tourist boards can always be contacted for advice. Their addresses and telephone numbers are given on page 62. The kinds of publication in which a property might be advertised are considered next. Libraries and newsagents, especially the larger ones, carry a range of newspapers, journals, catalogues and magazines and it is well worth perusing as many as possible before deciding where to place advertising.

Annual periodicals – There are several annual publications such as the *Farm Holiday Guide to Self-Catering and Furnished Holidays*. The Tourist Board's nationwide and regional publications are worth considering. They are well used, and, depending upon your area, are often well produced and a cost-effective place to advertise. Other publications specialise in certain types of property, such as farm cottages. The response rate to advertisements in these annuals varies enormously. Owners of several units, or expensive property, may do well to consider these annual publications, but note that most publishers require full details sometimes as early as June for release in the following year. For one small property only, it may well be more cost-effective using regional newspapers in a selected area.

Periodical magazines – These are well used by self-catering property owners. Some of these magazines, such as *The Lady*, have pages of advertisements for holiday lettings during the height of the booking period in February and March. The cost of advertising varies considerably, but is on the whole fairly high. There is a very wide range of choice, but some of the more unusual publications, such as the *Church Times* or the *Catholic Herald*, often produce the best results with the least expense. *Nursing Times* and *Farmer's Weekly* should also be considered. The National Trust magazine has a large readership throughout the United Kingdom and contains a number of advertisements for holiday accommodation to let. Depending on your area, an advertisement aimed at a more specialised readership might yield a good response; consider, for example, *Birds*, the magazine for members of the Royal Society for the Protection of Birds.

Regional periodicals – are expensive and the area should be chosen with care. This is really a matter of trial and error, but if you feel that your property would appeal especially to the type of reader as well as the area covered by such a magazine, then it may be worth a try.

National daily newspapers – It is not necessarily the case that the higher circulations enjoyed by the national daily press ensure any greater value for money. Beware the "hard sell" from newspapers' advertising staff, and don't be encouraged to spend more on advertising than you intend. Although the daily papers are effective, the Sundays may well be more so.

National Sunday newspapers – As with the daily newspapers, these papers have very large circulations and are generally expensive. However, if you have an up-market property, then a good, detailed, advertisement in *The Sunday Times* or *The Observer* for example, may be worth a try. A better response is generally obtained from a Sunday than a daily newspaper.

Regional or local newspapers and "Ad mags" – These are generally favoured. Advertising is comparatively cheap and the response is often quite reasonable. It is wise to consider the region with some care as readers in some areas seem to be more attracted to self-catering holidays than in others.

Advertising abroad – is risky for the inexperienced. Of the Europeans, the Belgians and the Dutch are most interested in self-catering holidays in the U.K. To attract overseas visitors it is often found best to locate a local agent through the tourist board in the country in question. The ETB in London can supply the address of the tourist authority in other countries. The English Tourist Board offices in Europe are particularly helpful. If advertising is placed overseas, it should ask that replies be sent to the local agent.

Town Council publications – Some town councils produce an accommodation register. It is often worthwhile to have holiday property listed, provided the cost is not prohibitive. It is prudent to ask the number printed to get some idea of the possible circulation.

(c) Taking bookings

Once advertising is under way, the responses should begin. The majority of people telephone for details; a few will write. Each enquirer should, of course, be encouraged to make a firm booking. This is where good preparation will pay dividends. There should be a pad near the telephone to take names and addresses of enquirers, and the bookings diary to check availability. The initial reaction on the telephone should be positive but moderate; if a booking can be secured from the initial telephone call, the inquirer should be asked to send written confirmation of the booking and a deposit cheque. If particulars have to be sent out or a letter answered, these matters should be dealt with promptly. Brochures should be sent by first class post as soon as possible. If the brochure is well prepared, the advertiser should be able to tell enquirers confidently that it contains all necessary details.

Once a booking is accepted, the owner should acknowledge receipt of the deposit and confirm that the dates requested are available, at the same time answering any queries which are raised. Once a clear booking has been taken, details of it should be kept in a diary near the telephone, to show at a glance the availability of the property. Great care should be taken to avoid double-booking. This is not only very embarrassing, but could also prove expensive – a landlord who has agreed to provide accommodation has a contractual obligation to do so, and will be in breach of contract if he fails to provide suitable alternative accommodation. Failure to find suitable alternative accommodation for the disappointed double-booked visitor, might result in paying for them to stay in a hotel.

As regards cancellation by the other party to the contract, it is useful to state in the particulars that on cancellation the deposit will be forfeit, and on cancellation within a month of the booked date of arrival, the full rent will be payable unless alternative occupiers can be found. An owner must attempt to mitigate his loss by re-letting. Technically, an owner who receives a last-minute cancellation is entitled to recover the whole of the rent due if he cannot find another occupant, but in practice this may be difficult to do. One of the advantages of having an agency is that they might help with such problems.

The addresses of the English Tourist Board and the regional offices are listed below:

Cumbria Tourist Board
Ashleigh
Holly Road
Windermere LA23 2AQ
Tel: (09662) 4444

East Anglia Tourist Board
Toppesfield Hall
Hadleigh
Suffolk IP7 5DN
Tel: (0473) 822 922

East Midlands Tourist Board
Exchequergate
Lincoln LN2 1PZ
Tel: (0522) 31521

The English Tourist Board
Thames Tower
Blacks Road
Hammersmith
London W6 9EL
Tel: (01) 846 9000

Northumbria Tourist Board
Aykley Heads
Durham DH1 5OX
Tel: (091) 384 6905

North West Tourist Board
The Last Drop Village
Bromley Cross
Bolton BL7 9PZ
Tel: (0204) 591 511

Thames and Chilterns Tourist Board
The Mount House
Church Green
Witney
Oxon OX8 6DZ
Tel: (0993) 778 800

West Country Tourist Board
Trinity Court
Southernhay East
Exeter EX1 1QS
Tel: (0392) 76351

Heart of England Tourist Board
2–4 Trinity Street
Worcester WR1 2PW
Tel: (0905) 613 132

London Tourist Board
26 Grosvenor Gardens
London SW1W 0DU
Tel: (01) 730 3450

Yorkshire & Humberside
Tourist Board
312 Tadcaster Road
York YO2 2HF
Tel: (0904) 707 961

---

6. Conversion of buildings to self-catering holiday units

Although conversion of buildings into holiday units cannot be dealt with in detail in this book, some mention is appropriate, in view of the high number of agricultural buildings now being granted planning permission for change of use to dwelling-houses. Broadly speaking, the stages in such a project are:

- assessing the viability and cost,
- preliminary planning,
- raising finance and grants,
- building works,
- decoration,
- equipping,
- marketing.

(a) Viability and cost

Before incurring costs, thorough consideration should be given to whether or not the project is viable. The first point of contact might be the development officer at the local branch of the English Tourist Board. Another source of advice is the Rural Development Commission (RDC) (formerly CoSIRA). Both can provide guidance on the viability of a project. The English Tourist Board provides a booklet, *Letting Holiday Properties*, price £3, and is recommended.

(b) Budgets

It is important in any business operation to set a business plan and subsequently to monitor information at regular intervals against that plan. Where a difference between the budgeted figures and the actual figures arises, an explanation should be sought if the difference is significant in value or percentage terms.

A *budget forecast* will contain various headings, eg income, wages, costs, under which expected income and expenditure figures are entered. The planned figures are then measured against actual performance figures as the business becomes operational.

Preparation of a budget – There are two types of forecast, the trading and the capital, which are combined to produce the cash flow budget. *The trading forecast* takes account of the income and expenses normally incurred, in order to arrive at the profitability of the operation. *The capital forecast* sets down the costs involved in setting up a business, which in general are non-recurring.

It may be more convenient when considering a holiday home operation to start with the capital budget on the presumption that a suitable property with a known purchase price has become available.

A feasibility study researching such factors as anticipated demand, whether the property is, or can be made suitable, whether planning permission is required (as in the case of a barn or outbuilding) whether its location is suitable, must all be considered in order to ensure that the proposal is viable in principle before any financial budgets are prepared.

Trading budget – The trading of the business must be successful in order to:

(a) pay for the overheads and direct costs incurred by the business;
(b) cover the loan interest;
(c) repay the loan instalments when due;
(d) provide a return to the proprietor for both time and capital invested.

(c) Preliminary planning

Working out the broad outline of a project calls for a fertile imagination, with a view to creating an interesting, attractive and comfortable development that is easy to manage. If there are to be multiple units (say five or more) it may be worth adding attractions, such as a tennis court, games room or restaurant, to entice visitors and improve income. A local architect or surveyor with some proven ability will initially advise generally on the number of units and provide a reaction to the project. If his ideas sound good and you are suitably impressed, ask to see some similar projects he has been involved with before instructing him. Architects' fees are high so it may be preferable to agree a fee structure which relates to actual time spent, rather than a percentage of the overall project cost.

Before incurring fees in preparing plans, it is wise to check that obtaining planning permission will not be a problem. A recent Government directive encourages the conversion of redundant barns to dwelling-houses, with or without a restriction for holiday use only. If barns or buildings are pre-1850, or are of architectural or historical interest, it may be appropriate to apply to have them listed. If you are successful then full planning permission should be granted, rather than a permission for holiday use only. Your property will be worth much more without the restriction to holiday use only.

If you wish to make enquiries yourself before consulting an architect, make an appointment with the local planning officer for him to meet you on site, and ask his views.

It is advisable to seek professional help when lodging the planning application and appropriate fees.

(d) Raising finance

Before attempting to raise finance a business plan and projections must be prepared. It is usual to seek professional advice, but there are some publications which will of be assistance. The ETB have produced a booklet – *How to Approach the Bank for Finance* – and there are other general publications on starting up a business which provide sound broad-based advice.

There are grants or loans available from either or both the Regional Tourist Board and the RDC, but funds are not released until the organisation in question is satisfied that the business will be viable and properly managed. Obtaining a grant is a very time-consuming procedure. Detailed projections and business plans will be required, and the assistance of an accountant may be needed. The policy of the local tourist boards is not to provide a grant unless the applicant can

Fixed overheads	Jan	Feb	Mar	Apr	May	Jun	Jul	Aug	Sep	Oct	Nov	Dec	Annual total
Heat and light	25	25	25	25	20	20	15	15	20	25	25	25	
Water rates	48	48	48	48	48	48	48	48	48	48	48	48	
Telephone and postage	10	10	8	8	5	5	5	5	5	5	8	8	
Repairs and renewals	–	–	–	–	–	–	–	–	–	–	–	200	
Accountancy	–	–	–	–	–	–	–	–	–	–	–	150	
Insurance	8	8	8	8	8	8	8	8	8	8	8	8	
Advertising	50	50	50	25	–	–	–	–	–	–	50	50	
Cleaning	40	40	40	40	40	40	40	40	40	40	40	40	
Total	181	181	179	154	121	121	116	116	121	121	179	529	2119
Rental income before interest (based on 40 weeks)	180	140	360	360	600	600	800	800	600	240	240	120	5040
Net profit (loss) before interest	(1)	(41)	181	206	479	479	684	684	479	119	61	(409)	2921

Example of trading budget for a holiday home

prove real need, and that he has tried to raise the money elsewhere without success. If successful, the grant may be as high as 25% of the total conversion cost, or £6,000 per unit, whichever is the lower.

An owner must register for VAT purposes when his taxable turnover exceeds £22,100 per annum, or £7,500 in any calendar quarter. The figures are before deducting expenses, and apply from 16 March 1988. If registered for VAT, the tax on conversion costs and later costs can be reclaimed, but VAT must be charged on rents. Newly-built accommodation is zero-rated.

(e) Building work

Selecting a reliable builder is not easy and the usual advice applies: it is as well to inspect work already done by the builders who are estimating; personal recommendations are valuable; and the lowest price does not always indicate the best builder. Building works are notorious for taking longer than planned, so it is as well to leave a realistic time gap between the date the building works are scheduled to be completed, and the date of the first booking.

(f) Decoration, equipment and marketing

All that has been said earlier in this chapter about decorating, equipping and marketing a holiday home of course applies to newly-built properties; see pages 49 to 55.

---

7. Community charge ("poll tax")

At the time of writing, the proposed community charge or poll tax has not replaced general rates, but it appears likely to do so in April 1990. Poll tax will be payable by all adults over eighteen living in this country, subject to some specific exceptions.

As far as second homes or holiday-let properties are concerned, the Government feels that it would provide an unfair windfall to those owners if no tax were levied. It is proposed that these properties should bear a standard charge equal to two units of community charge for the area. This will apply to all dwellings not occupied as a main residence, but with the exception of empty houses which are either uninhabitable or which are temporarily empty for up to three months.

The standard charge of two units is intended to be the same as existing rates, but it is also proposed that if a local authority considers that a standard charge equal to two units is excessive, it has a discretion to charge less. As far as caravans are concerned, special provision for a reduced charge is likely to be made.

5

Farm cottages

1. Introduction

In recent years the decline in the number of agricultural workers has resulted in there being many farm cottages left vacant. Rather than allow them to fall into disrepair, letting may be the most profitable and effective course. Holiday lettings have already been considered in Chapter 4; this market is considered difficult but a farm cottage can be successfully marketed in this way if it is in an especially desirable area and fitted to a high standard.

In addition to the general legal implications set out in Chapters 1 and 2, there are some special provisions which apply to farm cottages, and these are considered in this chapter.

Before a farmer decides to let a vacant property he should be aware that there are basically three types of letting which may apply to a farm cottage:

- a letting of a farm cottage to someone who is not an agricultural worker;
- a letting of a farm cottage to someone who is employed in agriculture;
- a letting of a farm cottage with agricultural land.

In the first of these, the tenant will be in the same position as any other tenant of property where the landlord is not resident. The second case is a special type of assured tenancy which gives rise to the "tied cottage". The third type of letting should be approached with care as it may fall outside the Housing Act altogether.

2. Lettings to tenants who are not employed in agriculture

If a farmer lets his cottage to someone who is not and has not been a farm worker, no special rules apply. Unless he lets on shorthold or on one of the particular types of tenancy provided by the Housing Act (see Chapter 2) the tenant will have security of tenure. Even if the farmer then finds that he needs the property to house farm workers, he will not be able to obtain possession unless he can prove one of the Grounds listed in Schedule 2 to the Housing Act. A farmer who wants to let his cottage and be able to regain possession of it at the end of the letting, has a choice of three courses:

- a holiday let
- a letting out of season for a maximum of eight months under Ground 3 if the property has been previously let for holiday purposes
- a shorthold let.

All of these possibilities are dealt with in previous chapters; see page 21 for holiday lettings; page 32 for out-of-season lettings; and page 23 for shortholds.

3. Lettings to farm workers

Most farmers are familiar with the expression "tied cottage". Since 1977, agricultural workers who have occupied a cottage as part of their employment have been given security of tenure by the Rent (Agriculture) Act 1976. Any letting which took place before 15 January 1989 is governed exclusively by the provisions of this Act, and legal advice should be taken if a farmer has existing tenants. If the worker or a member of his family continues to occupy the accommodation after his employment with the farmer has ceased (whether he has been made redundant, sacked or left of his own accord), the 1976 Act specifies the occupier's protection against being evicted.

The Housing Act 1988 continues to give agricultural workers

security of tenure and creates a new form of assured tenancy known as an *assured agricultural occupancy*. Unlike other assured tenancies, it does not matter if the tenant is charged a low rent, or even no rent at all – he is still protected by the Act.

A farm worker will enjoy an assured agricultural occupancy under the Housing Act if he is provided with accommodation by his employer and he is a "qualifying worker". This means that he must either:

(a) have worked full time in agriculture, or as a permit worker, for not less than 91 out of the last 104 weeks; during this time he need not necessarily have occupied the tied cottage in question; *or*

(b) be incapable of full time work by reason of injury sustained in the course of his employment in agriculture.

It is very important to note that the tenant does not gain any of this security if the letting is on shorthold, even if he is an agricultural worker.

The effect of this is that if a farmer permits one of his workers to occupy a farm cottage, and that worker has effectively spent the previous two years working in agriculture, the worker will have security of tenure. He cannot be evicted except on certain of the Grounds specified in the Housing Act which are set out below. It does not matter whether the letting is described as a tenancy or licence: so long as the worker does not share the property with the farmer or his family he will be treated as a tenant. Even if he leaves the farmer's employment he will still have the right to remain in the property until the farmer can establish a Ground for possession.

When a farm worker who has an assured agricultural occupancy dies, then the widow, widower or co-habitee can succeed to the tenancy if that person was living in the property immediately before the tenant's death. Where there is no surviving spouse or co-habitee, one of the members of the tenant's family can take over the tenancy so long as they have lived in the house for the previous two years. Whoever succeeds to the tenancy will then have the right to stay in the property until the farmer can establish one of the Grounds for possession.

It must be stressed that even where a worker himself gives notice to leave his employment he may still be entitled to an assured agricultural occupancy after he has left his job. Any farmer wishing to take on a new farm worker must be careful if he provides a tied cottage to go with the job. It is not impossible for a new employee to move into a tied cottage, perhaps with a large family, and then hand in his notice after a few days' work. If he has been an agricultural worker for the previous two years, the farmer is left with little choice but to go to his solicitor to obtain a court order to rehouse the worker in council accommodation. This is often a cumbersome, harassing and expensive process which involves the co-operation of the local housing authority. The local authority may have difficulty in providing suitable alternative accommodation for the farm worker, and if there is no accommodation available, then nothing can be done even if the tenant himself is anxious to be re-housed. It has also been known for a local council to refuse to offer accommodation on the basis that the farmer himself has alternative accommodation which could be used to rehouse the tenant, even where this property is too large, or is already occupied by the farmer's domestic employees.

(a) Grounds for possession

If a farmer wants to recover possession of a cottage, either to house another worker or for some other purpose, he *must* apply to the county court for an order for possession if the occupier refuses to leave. Under no circumstances should the farmer try to evict the occupier himself as he may well be guilty of a criminal offence under the Protection from Eviction Act 1977 and the tenant could claim damages against him.

Once court proceedings have been brought there are two possibilities:

(a) Where a farmer has granted his employee a shorthold tenancy he will be entitled to an order for possession at the end of the tenancy provided that he has served the correct notices and observed all the formalities (see Chapter 2).

(b) If a farmer has not let on shorthold, he has to prove a Ground for possession under Schedule 2 to the Housing Act before the court will grant an order.

The Grounds under Schedule 2 are set out in Chapter 1 (see page 9) and apply to an assured agricultural occupancy in exactly the same way as to an assured tenancy. The only Ground which does *not* apply to an assured agricultural occupancy is Ground 16, which entitles a landlord to possession of property which was let to a tenant in consequence of his employment where the tenant has ceased to be in that employment. As has already been explained, a farm worker is still entitled to remain in possession of his tied cottage even when his employment has ceased.

Grounds 1 to 8 of Schedule 2 to the Act are mandatory, that is the Court *must* order possession if the Ground is proved; while Grounds 9 to 15 are discretionary and the court has a choice as to whether or not possession should be granted. Most of the mandatory grounds are unlikely to apply to a farm cottage, and the farmer will probably have to rely on one of the discretionary grounds.

Before a farmer applies to the court for possession under one of the Grounds he *must* serve a notice on the occupier stating that he is seeking possession, and giving details of the Ground or Grounds he relies on. These notices have to be in a prescribed form, and a minimum notice period of two months is required. However, anyone who finds himself in this situation should *always* seek legal advice before taking any of these steps.

(b) Alternative accommodation for the assured agricultural occupier

A court may order possession of premises if suitable alternative accommodation is, or will be, available for the tenant when the order for possession takes effect (Ground 9 of Schedule 2 to the Housing Act).

In order to take advantage of this Ground, a farmer would have to provide his tenant with accommodation which is either similar to the sort of property the local authority would provide in the neighbourhood, or which is of a similar size and character to the property previously occupied. If furniture was provided in the previous dwelling then the new property must also be furnished in a similar fashion, or other suitable furniture provided. The accommodation must also be reasonably suitable for the needs of the tenant and his family and this includes its proximity to the tenant's work.

Where a farmer who wishes to obtain possession of his cottage cannot offer his tenant suitable alternative accommodation himself, and none of the other Grounds exist, he can apply to the local housing authority to rehouse the occupant of his tied cottage. So long as the local authority gives a certificate that it will provide suitable alternative accommodation by a certain date, a court will almost certainly make an order for possession.

A farmer wishing to rehouse a former employee or an existing one who is about to retire, can make an application to the local housing authority so long as he can prove:

(a) that he needs or will need vacant possession of his cottage in order to house somebody who is or is about to be employed on his farm;
(b) that he has no means of providing any suitable alternative accommodation; and
(c) that the local authority should "in the interests of efficient agriculture" provide suitable alternative accommodation itself.

To assist the housing authority in deciding whether or not it is in the interests of efficient agriculture to rehouse the occupant, a body has been set up called the Agricultural Dwellinghouse Advisory Committee (otherwise known as ADHAC). The housing authority, the landlord or the occupier can apply for an ADHAC to be appointed to consider the application and obtain its advice on rehousing applicants. Although the advice given is for assistance only and the housing authority is not bound to carry out the ADHAC recommendations, the landlord is entitled to see a copy of the advice and in some circumstances may challenge the authority's decision in the High Court.

One common reason which the local authority may give for refusing to rehouse a tenant is that the landlord himself can provide suitable alternative accommodation. The meaning of "suitable alternative accommodation" has caused some difficulty and is interpreted by local authorities in different ways. The Department of the Environment has provided some advice to authorities in the form of the Circular 122/76 Annexe A, para. 3, which states:

"In any particular case a decision as to whether the applicant can or cannot so provide is initially for the Housing Authority concerned. But the general intention underlaying the provision is that no rehousing duty can arise if the applicant can reasonably accommodate the worker or ex-worker in other suitable accommodation which is available or, in the case of advance applications, will be available at the time it is required. Such accommodation would either be owned by the applicant himself or else be accommodation in which he can house his workers because of special arrangements with someone else, such as a member of his family, a farming company with which he is associated or his landlord. An applicant, however, should not be expected to use accommodation which is temporarily empty because the worker has left and not yet been replaced, or because the accommodation is habitually used for seasonal workers or is let on a regular basis as a holiday accommodation, or which will be needed in the foreseeable future for a retiring worker who will have to be replaced. And similarly, the condition is not intended to extend to requiring applicants to try to find alternative accommodation in no way controlled by him. On the other hand there may be farm businesses where it would be appropriate to take account of the fact that cottages have been let outside agriculture, but that possession can be regained. . . ."

If the housing authority is satisfied that the landlord has made out the three grounds set out above, it must "use its best endeavours" to provide local authority accommodation. Time limits have been imposed on a local authority to give a decision on a rehousing application. If they seek advice from the ADHAC then they must give their decision within two months of the receipt of that advice. The ADHAC should give their advice within twenty-eight days of the request. These applications take some time, and if a farmer becomes frustrated with delays in the rehousing procedure, he should first press the local housing officer, then seek assistance from his local councillor and, if he is a member, contact the National Farmers Union.

If the occupier is offered accommodation by the local authority and does not accept it then the landlord will have to make an application to the court under Ground 9 and produce the local authority's certificate that suitable accommodation is available.

To summarise therefore, if a farmer requires his cottages for another employee he can apply to his local housing authority at the local council provided he can show all of the following:

- his house is let to an assured agricultural occupier within the Housing Act 1988;
- the present tenant is no longer an employee;
- the farmer requires vacant possession of the property to house a new employee;
- the farmer is unable to provide suitable alternative accommodation for the present tenant;
- the local authority ought, in the interests of efficient agriculture, to provide suitable accommodation itself.

4. Shorthold tenancies

A farmer who wants to make sure that he can obtain possession when a farm worker's employment finishes should seriously consider granting a shorthold tenancy. If a farm cottage is let on shorthold to an agricultural worker this prevents an assured agricultural occupancy from arising and the tenant will not have security of tenure. This can be a great advantage if a new worker is being employed and a farmer is unsure whether or not he will prove suitable.

The disadvantage of letting on shorthold is that a tenancy has to be for a minimum of six months and a proper notice in prescribed form must be served on a tenant beforehand. If a farmer then decides a worker is unsuitable he would not be able to get him out before the end of six months. However, this may be preferable to having to go through the lengthy procedure with the ADHAC, described above. If a worker *is* suitable, at the end of the six month period he can simply remain in possession paying rent as before and will continue to be a periodic shorthold tenant. The farmer can then obtain possession when he wishes by giving the tenant sufficient notice.

A shorthold tenancy cannot be used for existing occupants of tied cottages but is clearly worth considering when taking on a new farm worker.

5. Rent under assured agricultural occupancies

The position of an assured agricultural occupant as regards rent is basically the same as that of any other assured tenant (see Chapter 1). While a worker is employed on the farm there will not generally be any problems over rent, but difficulties may arise once his employment ceases. If the occupant either should not or cannot be evicted, the farmer may find himself with a sitting tenant who is paying a very low rent or possibly no rent at all. A worker who stays in the cottage after his employment has ceased has to continue paying whatever rent was previously agreed between himself and the landlord. If the occupant stops paying rent then the landlord could apply to the court for an order for possession under Grounds 8 or 10 (see page 12).

Where an occupant is paying his rent regularly, a landlord may wish to increase the rent, or change the terms of the tenancy. The steps which a landlord can take to increase the rent will depend on whether the tenancy was for a fixed term such as for six months; or was a periodic tenancy, weekly, monthly or quarterly, for instance. In either case it is always open to a landlord and an occupant to agree a new rent.

(a) Fixed term tenancies

Once a fixed term tenancy ends, an occupant goes on paying rent at the same rent and at the same intervals as before, and is known as a statutory periodic tenant. If no rent was payable under the original tenancy agreement, he will be treated as a monthly tenant, but he is not obliged to pay any rent until a new rent is either agreed or fixed. In both cases a landlord who wishes to vary the terms of the tenancy and have the rent altered has to serve notice on the tenant not later than a year after the ending of the fixed term tenancy. The tenant can do the same, and if no agreement is reached, either party has three months to refer the notice to the rent assessment committee which will fix the terms of the tenancy and also a market rent.

(b) Periodic tenancies

If an occupant was not granted a fixed term tenancy, but simply paid his rent at regular intervals, this will continue until his landlord serves a notice proposing an increased rent. A new rent cannot take effect any earlier than a year after the start of the tenancy and until at least a month has elapsed after the notice was served. Like any other assured tenant, an occupant has a right to refer the notice to the rent assessment committee which will fix a market rent unless the parties come to some agreement.

A farmer may be in some difficulty if a very low rent was agreed and an occupant gives his notice after a matter of weeks. The farmer could not serve a notice increasing the rent for at least a year and would have to accept the uneconomic rent until then. One way of avoiding this problem would be to enter into a tenancy agreement which contains a clause providing for increases of rent after certain periods, for example six months, of the tenancy. Alternatively it might be wise to grant a shorthold while the farmer sees whether the worker is going to stay or not.

6. Farm cottages let with agricultural land

This is a difficult area which must be approached with caution. The letting of agricultural land is generally subject to the special regime of the Agricultural Holdings Acts and a tenant in these circumstances may well have security of tenure. This type of letting falls outside the scope of this book and specialist legal advice is needed.

7. Planning conditions relating to farm cottages

Some farm cottages may be subject to an agricultural restriction, which means that when planning permission was originally granted it was conditional on the property being occupied by a person who is or was at some time employed in agriculture. To establish whether or not a property is subject to such a restriction, enquiries should be made of your local council. It is not easy to have these restrictions removed but much depends on the circumstances of the particular case and the policy of the local council. An agricultural agent should be contacted to advise if necessary.

6

Letting rooms in the home

A householder who wishes to let a room or rooms in his home to make extra income must consider which type of letting is most suitable for his circumstances, as well as appreciating the legal implications of any such letting. There is basically a choice between:

- providing "bed-and-breakfast";
- taking in a lodger who will have a room but share other accommodation with the rest of the family; or
- letting a bed-sitting room or other self-contained part of the house.

A feature of lettings by resident landlords is that a tenant or licensee will not have security of tenure, so the potential problem of sitting tenants does not arise. Even so, there are degrees of protection which may be given to a person who has a room or rooms in someone else's house.

First, a guest enjoying bed-and-breakfast on a short-term basis is generally a licensee and has no security whatsoever. He simply has a right to use the bedroom and bathroom. If he shares with the landlord's family accommodation such as the bathroom, dining room or sitting room, he will be what is known as an *excluded* licensee, who has no right to stay for longer than the period which has been agreed.

A lodger who has a room on a long-term basis and who either eats meals with the family, or shares some rooms in the house with them, is also an excluded occupier (whether he is legally a licensee or tenant), and can be asked to leave at short notice. A typical example of such a letting would be to students or to long-term "bed-and-breakfasters" who may be in receipt of supplementary benefit.

There may be an arrangement where rooms or a self-contained part of the house are let and the occupants do not share any accommodation (except perhaps the stairs or hall) with the householder or his family. Examples of this include the letting of a self-contained basement flat in a large house, and where several lodgers occupy rooms on a separate floor of the house and share a bathroom and kitchen between themselves. Generally these lettings will be treated as tenancies and the occupiers will have the right to a proper period of notice if the landlord wants them to leave. This means serving a written notice to quit in prescribed form which gives the tenant at least four weeks' notice.

If tenants or licensees in any of these situations refuse to leave the premises, a landlord must apply to the court for an order for possession and should not himself take any steps to evict, otherwise he may be liable to prosecution or a claim for damages.

1. Bed-and-breakfast

Although using rooms for bed-and-breakfast on a short-term basis does not strictly constitute *letting*, some mention is justified here, if only to present the reader with a possible alternative to letting. Some householders may find providing bed-and-breakfast convenient if the house is suitable to attract this kind of business.

Rooms should, if possible, have a washbasin and shaving point as this takes some of the pressure off the bathroom and will assist in the smooth running of the household.

(a) Planning permission

If a householder is proposing more than small scale bed-and-breakfast, he must consider whether or not planning permission is required from the local authority. It is a question of degree whether the carrying out of bed-and-breakfast would require planning permission. Each case must be dealt with on its own merits, taking into account the frequency of the commercial use as well as the proportion of the property to be used for bed-and-breakfast. Each local authority has its own guidelines, and the local planning officer will advise generally as to whether or not planning permission will be required in any particular case. A guest house or small hotel certainly requires planning permission. The appropriate forms for applying for planning permission can be obtained from the planning department of the local council. A relevant factor in obtaining permission if it is necessary, is that there must be sufficient car parking space, and this is often related to the number of bedrooms.

(b) Fire certificate and insurance

If there are more than a certain number of letting bedrooms it is necessary to contact the fire officer and obtain a certificate to state that the property conforms with the fire regulations. Often, detailed plans are required, showing rooms with exit point fire doors and so on, and an application fee will be payable. The insurance company should be told that the house is to be used for bed-and-breakfast so that any necessary adjustments to the policy can be made.

(c) Liquor licensing

If evening meals are going to be served to guests then it may be worthwhile providing alcohol with meals. If so, an application must be made to the local magistrates' court for a licence. It is generally wise to consult a solicitor, who will advise on the application, prepare and submit the various forms, and deal with the court hearing. Information about the type of licence required, the fee payable and the procedure to obtain a licence can be obtained from the office at the local magistrates' court.

(d) DSS bed-and-breakfast

Temporary accommodation for the homeless is in ever-increasing demand. Anyone considering providing this form of bed-and-breakfast should appreciate that although rooms may be kept filled, the running of such an establishment is different from the more traditional form of bed-and-breakfast.

There is no literature and few guidelines on this type of bed-and-breakfast. The rules differ from area to area. The first point of contact should be the local DSS office, to investigate local need, find out how many establishments there are in the area, and to check the going rate. It may be possible to discover the name of someone experienced in running such an establishment who might provide general advice and guidance.

A DSS claimant receives a separate cheque for a fixed amount to cover his lodging expenses and it is common practice for the claimant to endorse the cheque over to the owner. Payment may sometimes be late because of delays in processing social security claims, but the commonest problems for those providing this kind of accommodation is failure to receive payment at all. Unfortunately, the DSS is not able to pay the householder direct, and he cannot be reimbursed by the DSS if the guest fails to hand over the cash.

An owner is expected to provide a bed, some basic furniture and access to a bathroom and WC. It is usual practice to expect rooms to be vacated by 10.00 am and to re-admit guests at 6.00 pm, with the door finally locked at 10.00 pm. This may appear to be straightforward but it is certainly not easy to implement in practice. It is not humanely possible to eject some people on a cold or wet morning with nowhere to go and not well able to cope with the situation that has befallen them. Similarly it is impossible to ignore banging on the door after 10.00 pm. If guests refuse to conform to the house rules then they should be urged or told to find alternative accommodation.

It has become usual in some larger establishments catering specifically for DSS claimants to have rooms with individual electricity meters and basic cooking facilities. Often television sets are provided in the bedroom rather than having a television room, as the choice of programme is the most common source of disputes among guests.

Owners considering taking DSS claimants in their own homes should ensure as far as they are able that the prospective occupiers are suitable. The householder can pick and choose, and experienced DSS staff will be able to recommend certain claimants who may be more suitable than others.

While the majority of the homeless are of course perfectly properly behaved people in difficult circumstances, the business of providing them with accommodation should be approached realistically. Experience has shown that it is not easy to manage and should not be taken on by the faint-hearted.

It is regrettable that this section cannot be concluded without a warning about the security not only of the householder, but of other claimants as well. The owner's or caretaker's rooms should be locked at all times. All rooms should have a lock, the owner retaining a duplicate key. All guests should be warned to keep their rooms locked whenever they are unoccupied. If meters are fitted, they should be secured with a good quality padlock and emptied regularly. If a caretaker is employed to manage the establishment that person must be able to deal competently and firmly in the difficult situations which can arise.

From a legal viewpoint, this type of bed-and-breakfast provision will normally be treated as a licence and the occupant will not be entitled to security of tenure. If a landlord himself is resident on the premises there should be no problem, but once a landlord moves out and starts employing caretakers, he must appreciate that the line between tenants and licensees is a very narrow one. Where occupants have cooking facilities in their rooms and stay there all day, the court may classify them as tenants if it comes to possession proceedings. A landlord contemplating letting a whole house in this way, rather than having a few paying guests in his home, should take legal advice before he embarks on the scheme.

2. Letting a room to a lodger

Many householders with a spare room decide to take in a lodger to supplement their income or help pay the mortgage. This is practical if the house or flat is in an area where there are people looking for such accommodation. The local information centre (or the local authority) can advise generally on the local position, and may well suggest a suitable sort of tenant. If there is a university, college or polytechnic in the area, a student let for at least an academic term may be suitable. The accommodation officer should be contacted and will advise whether or not there are students looking for such accommodation, and the amount of rent usually paid. Lettings to students are often on a full board basis under which the householder provides evening meals and possibly mid-day meals at weekends.

The degree of protection against eviction which a lodger enjoys depends entirely on whether he is classified as an ordinary tenant/licensee or an *excluded* tenant/licensee. An excluded tenant/licensee is someone who shares accommodation with his landlord or the landlord's family, provided that the landlord or his family have always occupied the rest of the house as their only or principal home.

If a lodger is an excluded occupier (whether licensee or tenant), then a landlord can terminate his right to occupy by giving reasonable notice to leave. He does not have to take possession proceedings so long as the lodger can be persuaded to leave the premises peacefully. However, if a lodger does not leave when asked, then it is best to take legal advice since it is an offence to use force or the threat of force to secure entry to premises, or to harass a residential occupier.

Where a lodger does not share any room in the house with the landlord or members of the landlord's family, more formal steps have to be taken to obtain possession if the lodger does not leave when asked to do so. Legal advice should be sought, but a lodger must be given a written notice to quit in the prescribed form, which gives him at least four weeks to leave the property. Forms of notice with the prescribed information on them can be obtained from most legal stationers. If the lodger does not leave by the end of the notice period, possession proceedings will have to be brought in the local county court.

3. Letting part of a house

A householder who wishes to let a room or rooms in his house which are effectively self-contained, will almost certainly be granting a tenancy. If an occupier is given exclusive possession of at least one room, and does not share any other rooms with the landlord or his family, he will be entitled to a degree of protection from eviction whether the letting arrangement is described as a tenancy or licence.

However, so long as a landlord genuinely lives in the rest of the property himself, and fulfils the conditions set out below, he will be classed as a "resident landlord". This means that any tenancy which he might grant will not be an assured tenancy under the Housing Act 1988. The tenant will have no security of tenure and no right to apply to adjust the rent. The conditions which must be fulfilled by the landlord are as follows:

(a) only *part* of the house or flat may be let to the tenant;
(b) at all times since the date of the letting the landlord must have lived in the house or flat as his only or principal home;
(c) except where the landlord is letting part of a flat, the property must not be a purpose-built block of flats (ie, a landlord who lives in one flat in a block and lets another is *not* a resident landlord);
(d) the landlord must own the house or flat himself or with some other person (ie, the letting must not be by a property company);

(e) the landlord must not be letting to one of his tenants who previously had an assured tenancy of the same premises or of other premises in part of the same building.

These conditions will almost certainly be fulfilled by a householder who simply wishes to let a room or rooms in his own house. It does not make any difference that the rooms let are furnished or unfurnished, and the landlord can let out any number of rooms in the property so long as he remains in occupation himself. If a landlord does not live at the property, but simply keeps a room there for occasional use, then a tenant may well have security of tenure if the necessary requirements for an assured tenancy are met.

There have been many attempts in the past by non-resident landlords to give tenants the right to occupy rooms, on the basis that the tenant will not be entitled to any security of tenure and agrees to leave at the end of the term or after a specified period of notice. If a tenant has signed an agreement to this effect, but has exclusive possession of the rooms he occupies and there is no resident landlord, he may well be an assured tenant in spite of the agreement. He then cannot be evicted unless the landlord can prove one of the Grounds referred to in Chapter 2. A landlord who has more than one home and wishes to let rooms in one of the properties should take legal advice if he wants to be sure that he is not creating an assured tenancy.

It is always important to agree the rent to be charged and also to prepare a list of "house rules" which can be given to the occupier when he moves in. These may help prevent later conflicts over loud music, unwelcome pets or anything else which might prove disruptive. A model set of house rules is set out at page 138, and can be adapted to suit a landlord's own requirements.

If an occupier pays rent on a weekly basis, then the landlord is obliged to provide a rent book, unless the rent paid includes a substantial payment for board, such as where a lodger is provided with main meals.

There is no restriction on the amount of rent which can be agreed, and an occupier has no right to apply to a rent assessment committee to have the rent adjusted, although it is always open to the parties to agree a new rent between themselves.

Where a bed-sit or self-contained part of the house is let for a fixed term, the landlord should always enter into a written agreement with the tenant, and use one of the ordinary forms of tenancy agreement.

This will ensure that if problems arise before the end of the agreed term, the landlord can terminate the tenancy and seek possession of the premises.

If the letting is for a fixed term then a tenant is entitled to remain in occupation until the tenancy comes to an end and the term expires, unless the tenant has broken a condition of the tenancy agreement, when the landlord has the right to terminate the tenancy earlier.

If the letting is by the week or month with no definite term and the landlord wishes the tenant to leave, at least four weeks' written notice must be given. This notice is known as a notice to quit and *must* contain certain prescribed information which tells the tenant what his rights are. The prescribed information is as follows:

"1. If the tenant or licensee does not leave the dwelling, the landlord or licensor must get an order for possession from the court before the tenant or licensee can lawfully be evicted. The landlord or licensor cannot apply for such an order before the notice to quit or notice to determine has run out.

2. A tenant or licensee who does not know if he has any right to remain in possession after a notice to quit or a notice to determine runs out can obtain advice from a solicitor. Help with all or part of the cost of legal advice and assistance may be available under the Legal Aid Scheme. He should also be able to obtain information from a Citizens' Advice Bureau, a Housing Aid Centre or a rent officer."

Forms of notice which should contain this information are available from legal stationers. In the case of a letting for a fixed term, no notice to quit is required as the tenancy will come to an end on expiry of the agreed term.

If a tenant refuses to leave when either the tenancy or the notice to quit has expired, a landlord cannot personally evict him and must make an application to the court for an order for possession. So long as the landlord has given the tenant sufficient notice in the correct form, *and* can prove that he is a resident landlord, the court *must* grant an order for possession against the tenant. The court may postpone the date when the order comes into effect for up to six weeks, although usually the order is postponed for four weeks.

It should be noted that if a landlord evicts, attempts to evict or harasses the tenant in any way with a view to "persuading" him to leave without a court order, he may be committing a criminal offence. It is provided in the Protection from Eviction Act 1977 that it is an offence to try and drive out anyone (whether a tenant or a licensee) who has a right to occupy residential accommodation by any tactics which amount to harassment. There is also a new and additional right under the Housing Act 1988 for anyone who has been driven out of residential accommodation to bring an action for damages against the landlord and these can be very substantial indeed.

A householder considering letting a spare room to a stranger should consider how disruptive it will be to the running of the house, and whether he is prepared to accept that disruption. It is also wise to ensure, as far as possible, that the person selected is honest and reliable, and can pay the rent. It is not unreasonable to ask for references and for a deposit of up to two months' rent to cover the landlord against possible losses.

7

Tax

1. Income Tax

Income tax is payable on an individual's income, which includes rent received from property which is let. The amount of tax payable is calculated in two ways – under the Income and Corporation Taxes Act 1988 Schedule A or Schedule D Case VI, and is assessed under various schedules. Tax payable on income from land and property is assessed under Schedule A, which allows certain sums to be deducted from the income to arrive at the taxable income. In the case of a property that is let with furniture, the income arising is assessed under Schedule D Case VI. The rules relating to the assessment of tax under these two Schedules are outlined below.

(a) Schedule A – Letting income

The tax payable is assessed on the actual income received in the relevant tax year, that is the year which ends on 5 April. Thus, income received in the twelve months ending 5 April 1989 is taxed in the year 1988/89 and tax is payable on 1 January 1989. As the tax is payable before the actual income for the year may finally be known, the Inland Revenue will estimate the income and revise the assessment once the income tax return for the year ended 5 April 1989 has been submitted. The estimate is usually based on the previous year's rental income.

The taxable income from a property is calculated by determining the total income for the tax year and deducting allowable expenses. The main expenses which the Inland Revenue allow are:

(i)   repairs and redecorations both inside and outside the property (but not improvements);

(ii)   general and water rates and property insurance;

(iii) any rent payable on the property;

(iv) costs of maintaining gardens and cleaning;

(v)   any agent's collecting fees;

(vi) accountancy fees and certain legal fees;

(vii) deductions are also allowed for equipment used in the upkeep of the building and garden, such as vacuum cleaners and lawn-mowers which would be used for maintaining the common areas of the building.

The allowance against tax given in respect of expenditure on such equipment are known as "capital allowances". The whole of this capital cost is not allowed in full in the year the equipment was purchased, but 25% of the expenditure can be claimed as a writing down allowance in that year. The balance of the capital expenditure is carried forward to the next tax year and added to any further capital expenditure in that year, and so on until the capital cost has been exhausted. For example:

	£
Expenditure 1987/88	500
1987/88 Writing down allowance 25%	125
Written down value 5.4.88	375
Expenditure 1988/89	1,245
	1,620
1988/89 Writing down allowance 25% × 1,620	405
Written down value 5.4.89	1,215
1989/90 Writing down allowance 25%	304
Written down value carried forward 5.4.90	911

Deductions can also be made in respect of renewals of items of equipment; see page 90.

(viii) Interest charged on loans to finance the purchase or improvement of a property which is let are also allowable as a deduction from letting income, provided that the property is let at a commercial rent for more than 26 weeks in a year, and, when it is not so let, it is available for letting or is being repaired, improved or reconstructed. The amount of interest that can be allowed is restricted to the net income from letting, but any excess paid can be carried forward and set against the following year's profits.

Losses arising from letting a property may be carried forward and used against future profits from the same property. There are more detailed rules to allow certain letting losses to be set against profits from other properties, depending on the type of lease.

It is essential that where deductions are claimed, receipts should be kept as evidence of expenditure; they may at some time be required by the Inland Revenue as proof of payments made.

(b) Schedule D Case VI – Furnished letting income

Income from furnished letting is normally assessed on the "preceding year basis"; for example, the income received in the year ending 5 April 1988 will be assessed in the following year, 1988/89, and tax should be paid on 1 January 1989. The taxpayer may elect to have the proportion of the letting income which relates to the furniture taxed under Schedule D Case VI, and the balance taxed under Schedule A. This election must be made within two years of the assessment in question.

The expenses that are deductible from furnished letting income are the same as those listed for Schedule A (see page 89) with the exception of capital allowances on the furniture. In the place of capital allowances, the renewal of furniture and equipment is an allowable deduction, but not the initial expenditure on the equipment. The Inland Revenue allows an alternative to deductions for renewals in the form of a wear and tear allowance. This is calculated as 10% of the total rents received (after deduction of rates and other expenses which are normally borne by the tenants).

If services, such as laundry, or domestic help, are provided for the tenants the cost of these services are also allowable expenses.

For example, Mr and Mrs Brown own a cottage and, subject to a mortgage, a house in which they live. The Browns let the top floor of their house furnished, and let the cottage unfurnished. The calculations to be forwarded with their income tax return for the year ended 5 April 1989 are set out below:

Income:		*Schedule A*		*Schedule D VI*
		Lilac Cottage £		*Manor House* £
Rents received				
Furnished lettings				2,500
Unfurnished lettings		2,000		
Less Expenses				
Rates and water	480		360(⅓)	
Gardener's wages	260		–	
Repairs	140		310	
Fire insurance	100		90(⅓)	
Agents' commission	200		250	
Cleaner	–		80	
Wear and tear				
10% (2,500 – 360)			214	
Accountancy fees	30	1,210	30	1,334
Net Income		790		1,166
Interest paid on loan to purchase (⅓ × 3,000)		–		1,000
Taxable profit		790		166

Notes

1. As only the top floor of Manor House is let, only a proportion of the expenses relating to the entire property may be claimed. In the example it is assumed that one third of the floor area of the property is let and so only one third of the mortgage interest can be claimed. The allowable repairs are those specifically incurred on the let part of the house.

2. The profits will be assessed as follows:

	Year of assessment	*Tax payable*	*At basic rate* (25%)
Lilac Cottage – unfurnished	1988/89	1.1.88	£197.50
Manor House – furnished	1989/90	1.1.89	£41.50

(c) The taxation and treatment of furnished holiday accommodation

A taxpayer may treat income from commercial holiday lettings as a "trade" for tax purposes. The advantages of this are set out on pages 93 and 94. The accommodation to which this rule applies includes houses, cottages, flats, chalets and apartments or caravans but not properties overseas. The concession applies only to the "commercial letting" of furnished holiday accommodation, and not to lettings to students or any lettings generally. To qualify as a commercial letting for holiday purposes, four tests must be satisfied:

(i) The landlord must show that the accommodation is available for letting to the public as holiday accommodation for 140 days or more. The period does not have to be continuous, but it is essential that the property is available for letting for a total of at least 140 days in the tax year.

(ii) The property must actually be let to members of the general public as holiday accommodation for seventy days or more in the financial year. If two or more holiday properties are let, averaging may be used to enable more than one to qualify as "holiday accommodation" in respect of the seventy days letting rule. For example:

Property	*Number of days let as* *holiday accommodation*
Arden Cottage	95
Beach flat	60
Croft House	65
	220

Arden Cottage can be averaged with either Beach flat or Croft House, producing average lettings of seventy-seven and a half days and eighty days respectively. An election must be made by the taxpayer within two years of the year of assessment, as to which property – Beach flat or Croft House – is to have the benefit of averaging. Only one such election may be made in each year of assessment.

(iii) The landlord must let the property at a commercial rent, which must be the best rent he can reasonably obtain for the letting to be profitable.

(iv) The taxpayer must show that while the property is actually let for holiday purposes it is not normally in the occupation of the same person for a continuous period of more than thirty-one days during a period (not necessarily continuous) of seven months in the year.

The following example shows how accounts should be made up:

Seaview Cottage was let as follows during the financial year 1988/89:
April to October: to various holidaymakers on weekly and fortnightly lets – 22 weeks @ £60 = £1,320.
January to March: to Mr Parker, a local man, for 13 weeks @ £20 = £260.

Although the cottage has been let to Mr Parker for more than thirty-one days continuously, it will still be able to pass the "holiday accommodation" test as there is a period of seven months in the year within the period April to December when it was not let continuously for more than thirty-one days. The account to be submitted with the taxpayer's income tax return would be as follows:

		£
INCOME FOR THE YEAR ENDED 5 APRIL 1988		1,580
Expenditure		
Rates and water	415	
Insurance	50	
Wife's wages	720	
Cleaning materials	72	
Repairs and maintenance	110	
Renewal of equipment	41	
Accountancy	25	
Advertising	70	1,503
Net profit for the year		77

There are clear advantages for a taxpayer able to have his income from holiday lettings assessed under Schedule D Case I as income from a trade. These are briefly:

(i) Expenses can be off-set against income from any trade in arriving at the net profit, provided they are "wholly and exclusively" incurred in that trade. Thus, in addition to the expenses already mentioned, such as rates and insurance, other costs can be deducted. These might include wages to employees involved in the business (this may include the taxpayer's spouse); advertising and promotion expenses; postage; telephone calls; travelling and motor expenses incurred in the running of the business.

(ii) Certain tax benefits are available if the business is sold on retirement; see page 97.

(iii) Tax relief is also available if a property is sold and the cash reinvested; see page 97.

(iv) An individual who is not a member of a company pension scheme is allowed tax relief to purchase a retirement annuity. The retirement annuity payment made in a fiscal year is allowable against the taxpayer's earned income, subject to the amount of relevant income and the age of the taxpayer. As holiday lettings are a trade, the proprietors are able to make payments into such policies.

(v) If the business makes a loss over a tax year, this loss may be set against other income. If the loss occurs in the first three years of trading, this may be set against income of the previous three tax years, and may result in a refund of tax previously paid.

(vi) Tax is payable in equal instalments in January and July, based on the taxable profits of the business accounting year ending in the previous year ended 5 April. For example, a business which ended on 30 April 1988 falls within the tax year 1988/89, and is taxed in the following year – 1989/90 – with the tax payable in equal instalments on 1 January 1990 and 1 July 1990. The provisions relating to furnished holiday accommodation are somewhat detailed and any individual should seek the advice of a qualified accountant.

(vii) The trade may be arranged to be in the wife's name and if she has no other income the wife's earned income allowance (£2,785 – 1989/90) can be utilised against the income.

(d) Records

It is essential to keep a record of all income and expenditure incurred in relation to all lettings. The records should show to whom payments have been made and from whom they received details of the nature of the transactions. Most stationers will be able to supply cash books in which to record this information. Some record books set out headings and allow space in which the cash and the bank account can be reconciled.

It is important to keep receipts or vouchers to support the records. If an accountant prepares the accounts, well-kept records will help keep the cost down.

For example Honeysuckle and Rose Cottages are both owned and both are let fully furnished. Both qualify for tax purposes as furnished holiday lettings, and each cottage is let for thirty weeks at £150 per week. The accounts would be as follows:

	£	£
Income		
Honeysuckle Cottage		
(30 weeks @ £150)		4,500
Rose Cottage (30 weeks @ £150)		4,500
		9,000
General and water rates	1,750	
Garden upkeep	400	
Insurance	350	
Wife's wages	1,600	
Cleaning materials	320	
Repairs and maintenance	1,220	
TV hire and licence	570	
Accountancy	150	
Motor expenses	310	
Brochure costs	100	6,770
Net profit for the year		2,230
Less Capital allowance		400
Taxable income		1,830

2. Capital Gains Tax

(a) Liability to tax

Property that is used for letting will be liable to capital gains tax (CGT) on the "gain" when the property is disposed of. The "gain" is the difference between the sale proceeds after deduction of selling costs and the "base cost" as increased by an indexation allowance. For disposals after 5 April 1988 the "base cost" is the cost of the property and any improvements; or the value at 31 March 1982 if owned on that date and the cost of any subsequent improvements. The base cost is increased by an indexation allowance which is intended to index link the cost of the property in order that capital gains are not paid on normal inflationary increases in property values. Unfortunately, the index is based on the retail price index and not on a property price index.

The rate of CGT varies depending on the individual's income tax liability. The capital gain is added to the other income, and taxed at 25% and 40% subject to an annual exemption per couple of £5,000 (1989/90). For example:

	£	£
The Myrtles flat		
Sale proceeds 4.1.89		60,000
Less Sale costs – legal expenses	600	
estate agents fees	1,200	1,800
		58,200
Basic cost: Value at 31.3.82	25,000	
Indexation allowance	7,500	
Extension cost – 1987	4,000	
Indexation allowance	400	36,900
Gain		21,300
Less annual allowance (1988/89)		5,000
Gain subject to Capital Gains Tax		16,300
CGT @ 40%		6,520

The example assumes the taxpayer has an income that fully utilises basic rate income tax band.

(b) Let residences

A taxpayer's personal residence that has been used wholly or partly for letting can qualify for a £20,000 reduction in the gain applicable to the proportion of the building which was let.

(c) Retirement relief

This capital gains tax relief relates to business property only and is therefore relevant to furnished holiday lettings. When all, or a major part, of the business is disposed of by an individual aged sixty or over, at a gain, and the business had been owned for at least the previous twelve months, then, subject to certain conditions, an allowance against capital gains tax up to a maximum of £125,000 and 50% of the gain between £125,000 and £500,000 can be obtained. Both husband and wife, if trading in partnership, may claim retirement relief.

In order to qualify, the property sold must be part of the business and not just property held for investment purposes. It would be advisable to seek professional advice before the sale to ensure all the conditions are met.

The following is an example of how the retirement relief provision works:

Mrs Wheeler has owned two houses that qualified as furnished holiday accommodation before disposal in 1989/90.

	£	£
Net sale proceeds		400,000
Cost 1.4.85	140,000	
Indexation – say	35,000	175,000
		225,000
Annual allowance		5,000
		220,000
Retirement relief exemption 125,000		
and 50% × (220,000 – 125,000) 47,500		172,500
Chargeable gain		47,500
CGT @ 40% (say)		19,000

(d) Re-investment (CGT)

As furnished holiday lettings are classed as a business, the capital gain

on the disposal of certain property used in such a business may be
"rolled over" if another property is acquired to be used in a replacement
business, not necessarily furnished holiday lettings. The gain on
disposal of the original property is deducted from the base cost of the
new property for calculating the gain on the future disposal. If an
amount equal to sale proceeds is not re-invested, the rollover relief is
restricted.

The taxpayer has up to three years to re-invest in order to obtain this
valuable relief. It is not available to let property taxed under Schedule A
or Schedule D Case VI. Rollover relief can be a very important tool in
tax planning; it may even be possible, depending on circumstances, to
rollover a gain until the taxpayer is sixty years old, and then claim
retirement relief.

---

3. Value Added Tax

Letting of land is as a general rule, exempt from V.A.T., but the
regulations specifically provide that the provision of holiday accommodation in the form of a house, cottage, flat, caravan or houseboat is
liable to V.A.T. The letting of furnished accommodation for out of
season lettings in recognised holiday resorts for more than four weeks at
a time may be exempted from V.A.T. like ordinary rents, but the out of
season rent must be lower than the rent received during the season. For
more details of V.A.T. see Customs and Excise leaflet number 709.

From 14 March 1989 the annual turnover threshold at which the
taxpayer becomes liable to charge V.A.T. was raised to £23,600. If the
taxpayer is self-employed as a sole trader, for example if he is a grocer,
and is registered for V.A.T., the income from his holiday lettings will
still be liable for V.A.T., as both "businesses" are owned by the same
proprietor. If however, the holiday cottage was owned by the grocer
and his wife, this would represent a partnership between the couple,
and, therefore, under separate ownership for V.A.T. purposes; if the
income from the holiday cottage does not exceed the threshold of
£23,600 then no V.A.T. is either chargeable or payable.

4. Inheritance Tax

Inheritance tax is a tax on the value of an individual's estate after death; and on "chargeable transfers" made during a person's lifetime.

The rules relating are complicated, but, basically, from 5 April 1989 the first £118,000 of an individual's estate is free from inheritance tax and the remainder is liable to tax at a rate of 40%. If, however, the estate is bequeathed to the spouse, the transfer is exempt. This rule also applies to gifts to a spouse during a person's lifetime.

Gifts during an individual's lifetime are potentially liable to inheritance tax because if the individual dies within three years of the gift it is added back to his estate at death. A tapering relief is given for gifts made between three and seven years of death, so that gifts made more than seven years before death are exempt from inheritance tax.

It is important that individuals with assets over £118,000 should seek professional advice in order to mitigate liability to inheritance tax.

The following example shows how inheritance tax works:

Mr A died on 1 February 1989, leaving a house valued at £100,000 and investments worth £60,000. By his Will, he left his entire estate to his wife. Mrs A died on 1 April 1990, leaving her estate to the only child of the family. Inheritance tax would be payable as follows:

1. Mr A's death –
   £160,000 transfer to wife NIL (as a transfer to spouse)

2. Mrs A's death –
Value of estate	£160,000
Exempt	£118,000
Chargeable transfer	£42,000
Inheritance tax at 40%	£16,800

If Mr A bequeathed £42,000 of his investments to his child on his death the following result would have been achieved:

1. Mr A's death –
   £118,000 transfer to wife –   NIL   (transfer to spouse)
   £42,000 transfer to child –   NIL   as under £118,000
   exemption

2. Mrs A's death –

Value of estate	118,000
Exempt	118,000
	NIL
Inheritance tax	NIL

Furnished holiday letting businesses should qualify for "business property relief" – an inheritance concession which reduces the value of a chargeable transfer by up to 50%.

5. The Business Expansion Scheme

Under the business expansion scheme, introduced in 1983, income tax relief on money invested is available to individuals subscribing for eligible shares in a qualifying company. Basically, relief is given up to a maximum of £40,000, by setting the amount subscribed for shares against the individual's income, thereby reducing income tax liability. Detailed rules apply to the scheme, and certain specialist firms now market business expansion scheme funds, whereby the investor purchases shares in the fund which may be spread over many qualifying companies.

Companies specialising in the provision of qualifying assured tenancies over a period of at least four years from the date they issue shares qualify for business expansion scheme status. This extension of the scope of the scheme, now enacted in the Housing Act 1988, will allow investors to obtain tax relief (up to 40% in 1989/90) on an investment into a company backed by freehold property investments.

6. Rents payable to person living abroad

Where the landlord lives abroad and employs an agent in the United Kingdom to collect rents and manage the property, the tenant pays the whole of the rent to the agent without any deductions. The agent must deduct basic rate tax from the payments made to the overseas resident. If the tax, deducted at source, exceeds the actual tax liability after expenses are claimed, then the landlord should claim a repayment of tax. Application forms are available from the local Inspector of Taxes. The agent must pass all tax he has collected to the Inland Revenue.

If the tenant pays rent direct to the overseas landlord, then the tenant must deduct tax at the basic rate and pay it over to the Inland Revenue himself.

The purpose of these rules is to collect at source tax due from a taxpayer whose "usual place of abode is abroad". If the taxpayer is in doubt whether this rule applies he should contact his local Inspector of Taxes.

7. Collection of tax from the tenant or agent direct

The Inland Revenue has power to collect tax direct from a tenant, sub-tenant or from the landlord's agent if the landlord fails to pay tax on Schedule A income himself, and is not in occupation of the particular property.

The Inland Revenue may require the tenant to pay over rent as it falls due in satisfaction of arrears of tax. These payments release the tenant from his obligation to pay rent to his immediate landlord. If the tax is collected from a sub-tenant, then the rent withheld from his immediate landlord will be treated as a payment of tax by that landlord which he in turn is entitled to deduct from the rent that he pays any superior landlord.

If a taxpayer employs an agent to collect his rents, the Collector of Taxes may require any rents or other Schedule A income due to the taxpayer to be paid direct to the Inland Revenue if there are outstanding tax obligations. Any necessary expenses for which the agent may be liable, such as his own expenses and rates, can be deducted first, before the balance is forwarded to the Collector. If there is any doubt, then the agent should clarify the matter by contacting the local Tax Office. If an agent fails to comply with a notice served on him by the Collector of Taxes, he is liable to a financial penalty for each failure to comply.

The Inland Revenue, as is well known, has very wide powers; these extend to requiring tenants or agents to give details of any tenancy, which includes the name and address of the landlord and the person who collects the rent; information about the lease itself; and the occupation and use of the property. In addition, an agent may be required to supply details of rents he has collected and payments made.

8

Trouble-shooting

1. Checklists

There are two cardinal rules for avoiding trouble in the first place: DO seek legal advice and DON'T delay. Many problems are exacerbated by failure to find out the legal position and by delay in taking action. Landlord and tenant law is notoriously difficult even for lawyers, and although this book aims to help landlords avoid some of the worst pitfalls, it is always prudent to take legal advice. This applies particularly if letting property where the landlord is not resident.

If a problem crops up, the landlord should not let matters ride. If the tenant is in arrears with the rent, or has allowed someone else to occupy the property without the landlord's consent, it is vital to take action at once. The classic example of undue delay is the case of a squatter who is allowed to stay in a property. Once a squatter has been in uninterrupted occupation for more than twelve years he may actually become the *owner* of it!

Apart from these two basic rules there are a number of other "do's" and "don'ts" which may prevent difficulties from arising:

DO

- Choose your tenant with care and follow up references. It is unwise to let to friends of friends without proper references, particularly an employer's and bank reference. Remember to take a breakage deposit.
- Avoid initial uncertainty. Make sure you have a properly drafted

tenancy agreement which contains all the terms you want to put in. Agree an inventory of furniture and effects to be attached to the agreement.

- Take legal advice if you are in doubt about your position rather than the advice of well-meaning friends.
- Check your lease if you are letting a flat or maisonette as there may be a restriction on letting.
- Serve the correct notice in prescribed form *before* entering into an assured shorthold tenancy.
- Keep receipts and a properly organised filing system. Your accountant will provide some guidance if required.
- Have someone on hand for holiday lets in case there is a problem.
- Remember that once you have let property to a tenant you will have limited rights of access to the property. You cannot go in and out as you like.
- Make sure that the property is fully insured and that the insurance company is aware that the property is let.

DON'T

- Let a property (except a short-term holiday let) without a written tenancy or licence agreement.
- Let a tenant into possession of property before signing the agreement.
- Take on a tenant unless you are as satisfied as you can be that the tenant is suitable. You should not take on someone simply because you feel sorry for them.
- Delay in taking action if you are concerned about anything.
- Charge an unrealistic rent for a property.
- Embark on holiday letting without making sure that your property and the area are suitable. You should not let property unless it is of an appropriate specification or visitors are aware of any short-comings. The standard expected is generally higher than for an ordinary tenancy.
- Let a property under an assured tenancy if you want the property back at the end of the tenancy. Consider letting on an assured *shorthold* tenancy.
- Allow rent to get into arrears – be firm.
- Harass a tenant or attempt to evict him yourself – you may be sued for damages.

2. If things go wrong

There are bound to be some difficulties in the course of letting property. Once something has gone wrong it is important to remember three things:

- Don't ignore it.
- Don't delay.
- Don't hope it will resolve itself!

Usually, the landlord will need to take legal advice as soon as possible. It is wise to do so rather than taking action oneself, which could make matters worse. A number of common problems arise because of the actions of the tenants, the actions of the landlord or the actions of outsiders. These are discussed briefly below.

(a) Non-payment of rent

If the tenant is in arrears with the rent or is in the habit of paying late, this can be a Ground for possession (see page 12). The landlord will have to go to court to recover the rent owed, and should make sure that there are accurate records (such as a rent book) to show non-payment. Where there are arrears of rent which exceed certain specified amounts, a court must grant a possession order (see Chapter 1). Even if the arrears are not large enough to *ensure* that an order must be made, it may be worthwhile serving a notice seeking possession. Where a tenant is a bad payer and is either frequently late paying his rent, or allows arrears to build up, a court often makes a "suspended" possession order. This allows a tenant to stay in occupation as long as he continues to pay the rent plus a regular amount off the arrears.

Sometimes there may be very good reasons such as ill-health or unemployment, why a tenant cannot pay. However, it should be borne in mind that it is easy for large arrears to accumulate, and if court action is then necessary to recover possession, the result could be heavy legal expenses and no means of recovering them or the arrears from an impoverished tenant.

(b) Damage to property or furniture

This can also be a Ground for possession, although a court may be reluctant to order possession of the property unless the damage is fairly serious. If the landlord is concerned about the state of the property, he should take advice and check the position under the tenancy agreement. It may be wise to arrange to inspect the property and take photographs or make detailed notes on the state of repair, although this can be easier said than done. If there is an inventory it is a good idea to check through it and to find out the value of any damaged items. A landlord under an assured tenancy is entitled to have access to the property in order to carry out those repairs for which he is responsible, but this should be done only after at least twenty-four hours' written notice has been given to the tenant.

(c) Sub-letting

Tenants who have assured periodic tenancies are not allowed to let all or part of the property to anyone else without the landlord's consent. This will also be the case in any other kind of tenancy where there is a clause in the agreement which prevents sub-letting. If it is suspected that the tenant has left and someone else is in occupation the landlord should not accept any rent or enter into any agreement with them without taking legal advice. It will be necessary to go to court to get an order for possession of the property and this should be done as soon as possible.

(d) Squatters

Squatters used to strike fear into the hearts of landlords and they can still be a real problem, particularly in large cities where any empty property is almost immediately a target. Fortunately, there is a relatively quick procedure for evicting squatters through the courts and any solicitor should be able to advise about this. Prevention is clearly better than cure, and it is sensible to keep vacant property looking "lived in" and to make sure someone visits it regularly. Even though squatters have no legal right to remain in property, it is an offence to use force to evict them.

(e) Unwanted tenants or licensees

Tenants who refuse to leave when their tenancy comes to an end are a frequent problem, mainly because of the housing shortage and the refusal of local authorities to offer accommodation until a court order is made. There is no solution except to serve a notice of proceedings for possession and go to court. A landlord who tries to evict his tenants or licensees by any other means runs the risk of being sued for damages. The Housing Act allows a residential occupier to claim damages which are based on the difference between the value of the property with the occupiers in residence and its value without them. This could be a very large claim indeed.

Appendix 1

Forms

---

1. Model tenancy agreement

This form may be used, with adaptations to suit the particular case, for an assured or non-assured tenancy other than an assured shorthold.

AN AGREEMENT made the   day of
  19   BETWEEN [*type in name of landlord*] of [*and his address*] (hereinafter called "the Landlord") which expression shall where the context so admits include the person for the time being entitled to the reversion immediately expectant on the determination of the tenancy hereby created) of the one part and [*proposed tenant's name*] of [*and address*] (hereinafter called "the Tenant") of the other part.

  WHEREAS
[*insert here the appropriate notice; see pages 111 to 113*].

  WHEREBY IT IS AGREED as follows:

1. THE Landlord agrees to let and the Tenant agrees to take the *dwellinghouse/flat known as and situate at [*insert address of property to be let*] (hereinafter called "the premises") together with the fixtures, furniture and household effects now in the premises and listed in the Schedule (hereinafter called "the furniture") for a term of commencing on the   day of
  19 [and terminating on the   day of

19   ] [OR and thereafter from month/year to month/year until the tenancy hereby created shall be determined by either party giving to the other at least   notice in writing to quit the premises] AT A RENT OF £   per calendar month in advance, the first payment to be made on the signing of this agreement.

2. THE TENANT AGREES with the Landlord as follows:
(i)   To pay the rent at the times agreed herein.
(ii)   To pay for all electricity, gas consumed and telephone charges made and standing charges made during the tenancy.
(iii) To preserve the interior of the premises in good clean and substantial repair and condition.
(iv)   To preserve the furniture and effects from destruction or damage, to keep the furniture in good and clean condition (damage by accidental fire and reasonable wear and tear excepted; to immediately pay the Landlord the value of replacement of any furniture or effects lost damaged or destroyed or at the option of the Landlord replace immediately any furniture or effects lost damaged or destroyed and not to remove or permit to be removed any furniture or effects from the premises.
(v)   Not to make any alterations or additions to the premises without the consent of the Landlord.
(vi)   Not to carry on any business, trade or profession on or from the premises or receive any paying guests on the premises or use the premises otherwise than as a single *dwellinghouse/flat.
(vii) Not to exhibit any notice or advertisement upon or near the premises or to do or permit to be done anything which may or shall cause nuisance, annoyance, inconvenience or disturbance to the Landlord or to any adjoining or neighbouring occupier.
(viii) Not to assign, sublet, or part with possession of the premises or any part thereof.
(ix)   Not to keep any pets or animals on the premises or any part thereof.
(x)   To permit the Landlord or his authorised agent to enter on the premises at all reasonable times in order to examine the state of condition thereof and with reasonable notice to carry out works of maintenance or repair.
(xi)   To preserve and maintain the general character of the garden in a reasonable manner according to the season and not to cut down,

lop or remove any tree, shrub or plants growing on or near the premises.

(xii) To maintain the state of decoration of the premises to a standard reasonably acceptable to the Landlord or his agent and not to use different colour schemes without the Landlord's written consent.

(xiii) To yield up the premises at the expiration or sooner determination of the tenancy together with all the said furniture and effects in the same clean state of condition as they shall be in at the commencement of the tenancy.

3. THE TENANT FURTHER AGREES to deposit with the Landlord/his agent the sum of £   to be held against dilapidations, breakages, unpaid accounts, incidental costs for which the Tenant may be liable under this Agreement so that the deposit or any balance thereof shall be refunded to the Tenant on termination of the tenancy, but shall not be treated as rent or relieve the Tenant of the obligation to make full payments of rent.

4. THE LANDLORD AGREES with the tenant as follows:

(1) Provided the Tenant shall pay the rent and perform the agreements on his part hereinbefore referred to, the Landlord shall permit the Tenant to have quiet enjoyment of the premises without lawful interruption by the Landlord or his agent.

(2) To pay all rates in respect of the premises save for all charges for gas, electricity and telephone.

5. If the rent shall remain unpaid for more than 14 days after the same has become due (whether legally demanded or not) or if the Tenant shall fail to observe or perform any of the stipulations contained in paragraph 2 hereof it shall be lawful for the Landlord to re-enter upon the premises and the tenancy hereby created shall come to an end without prejudice to any rights of action for arrears of rent or damages in respect of any breach of this agreement.

AS WITNESS the hands of the said parties hereto the day and year first above written.

SIGNED by the above named

*Landlord/Tenant in the presence of: [Landlord/Tenant signs here]

[Witness signs here,
giving address and
occupation]

*Delete where inapplicable

Schedule
FURNITURE AND EFFECTS LET WITH THE PREMISES
[leave a good space here for inventory]

Notices to be inserted into the tenancy agreement

As explained in Chapters 1 and 2 (see pages 9 to 11 and 31 to 33), it may
be necessary to give notice about Grounds for possession before the tenancy
commences. Forms of notice for Ground 1 (owner-occupier letting his/her
home); Ground 2 (letting a mortgaged property); and Ground 3 (out of
season holiday lettings) are given below. The appropriate notice may be
selected and inserted into the tenancy agreement as indicated on page 108, or
given to the tenant as a separate document.

(a) Ground 1: owner-occupier letting his/her home

The following words may be incorporated into the tenancy agreement:

WHEREAS the dwelling known as [address of property to be let] is
hereby let by the landlord being the owner-occupier of the premises
under the provisions of Ground 1 in Part 1 of Schedule 2 to the
Housing Act 1988, and NOTICE IS HEREBY GIVEN to the
Tenant that possession of the property may be recovered by the
Landlord under the said Ground 1.

Although it is recommended that a tenancy agreement, containing the
appropriate notice, is used, if there is no agreement, or if it does not
include the notice, a separate notice may be given as follows:

NOTICE IS HEREBY GIVEN under the provisions of the Housing Act 1988 that possession may be recovered under Ground 1 Part 1 of Schedule 2 of the said Act.

DATED this day of 19	Received a notice of which the foregoing is a copy.
	Signed ....
Signed .... Owner	Proposed Tenant

(The landlord signs one copy and the tenant another. The landlord then keeps the one signed by the tenant and *vice versa*.)

(b) Ground 2: letting a mortgaged property

The following clause may be incorporated into the basic form of tenancy agreement:

WHEREAS the dwellinghouse known as [*name and address of property*] which is hereby let by the landlord is at the date hereof subject to a mortgage and NOTICE IS HEREBY GIVEN to the Tenant that possession may be recovered under Ground 2 Part 1 of Schedule 2 to the Housing Act 1988.

A notice may still be given to the tenant independently of a tenancy agreement:

NOTICE IS HEREBY GIVEN under the provisions of the Housing Act 1988 that the property known as [*name and address of property*] is subject to a mortgage and possession may be recovered under Ground 2 Part 1 of Schedule 2 to the Housing Act 1988

DATED this day of 19	Received a notice of which the foregoing is a copy.
	Signed ....
Signed .... Owner	Proposed Tenant

(The landlord signs one copy and the tenant another. The notices are then exchanged.)

(c) Ground 3: out of season holiday let

This ground applies where a dwelling has been let for a holiday at any time within the period of twelve months immediately before the commencement of the letting to a tenant for non-holiday purposes for a period not exceeding eight months:

> WHEREAS the dwelling known as [*name and address of property*] which is hereby let by the landlord has at some time within the period of 12 months ending on the date of this Agreement been occupied for holiday purposes NOTICE IS HEREBY GIVEN to the Tenant that possession may be recovered under Ground 3 Part 1 of Schedule 2 to the Housing Act 1988.

A notice may still be given to the tenant independently of a tenancy agreement. A simple form of notice would be as follows:

> NOTICE IS HEREBY GIVEN under the provisions of the Housing Act 1988 that at some time within the period of 12 months ending on the date of commencement of this tenancy the property known as [*name and address of property*] has been occupied for holiday purposes and possession may be recovered under Ground 3 Part 1 Schedule 2 to the Housing Act 1988.

DATED this   day   Received a notice of which
of   19   the foregoing is a copy.

Signed ....   Signed ....
    Owner   Proposed Tenant

(The landlord signs one copy and the tenant another. The notices are then exchanged.)

---

2. Agreement for assured shorthold tenancy

(a) Reminders about shorthold

(i)   The term must be for a period of not less than six months.
(ii) The landlord has no right to bring the tenancy to an end before

the expiry of the agreed term except in the event of a breach of the agreement by the tenant, and then the landlord must institute court proceedings to recover possession.

(iii)   The landlord is always liable to maintain the exterior, structure of the property and the installations, such as sinks, pipes and drains.

(iv)   In order to recover possession at the end of the term the landlord *must* before the expiry date of the tenancy, give the tenant a written notice (a letter would suffice), which must state that the tenant has two months' warning from the giving of the notice to give up possession, and proceedings may then be brought under s 21 of the Housing Act 1988.

(v)   Before the agreement is signed a notice, NOTICE OF AN ASSURED SHORTHOLD TENANCY (see page 132) *must* be given to the tenant.

(vi)   Two copies of the agreement are prepared and each party signs one copy. The landlord retains the copy signed by the tenant. The tenant retains the copy signed by the landlord. The documents may need to be "stamped", see page 45. Also, the Schedule of furniture and effects should be signed by the tenant.

(b) Specimen shorthold tenancy agreement

AN AGREEMENT made the   day of
19   BETWEEN [*type in name of landlord*] (hereinafter called "the Landlord" which expression shall where the context so admits include the person for the time being entitled to the reversion immediately expectant on the determination of the tenancy hereby created) of the one part and [*proposed tenant's name*] of [*and address*] (hereinafter called "the Tenant") of the other part.

WHEREBY IT IS AGREED as follows:

1.   The Landlord agrees to let and the Tenant agrees to take the dwelling/flat known as [*insert name of property being let*] and situate at [*and address*] (hereinafter called "the premises") together with the fixtures furniture and household effects now in the premises and listed in the Schedule (hereinafter called "the furniture") for a term of   year(s) [6 months minimum] commencing on the   day of   19   and expiring on the   day of   19   AT A RENT OF £   per calendar month in advance the first payment to be made on the signing of this agreement.

2. It is intended that the tenancy created by this Agreement is and shall be an ASSURED SHORTHOLD TENANCY within the meaning of Section 20 of the Housing Act 1988 and subject to Part 1 of the said Act, and the Tenant acknowledges that the Landlord has given the Tenant a valid notice for the purposes of subsection (1) (c) of Section 20 before this Agreement was entered into.

3. THE TENANT AGREES as follows:

(i)   To pay the rent at the times agreed herein.

(ii)   To pay for all electricity, gas consumed and telephone charges made and standing charges made during the tenancy.

(iii)   To preserve the interior of the premises in good clean and substantial repair and condition.

(iv)   To preserve the furniture and effects from destruction or damage, to keep the furniture in good and clean condition (damage by accidental fire and reasonable wear and tear excepted); to immediately pay the Landlord the value of replacement of any furniture or effects lost damaged or destroyed or at the option of the Landlord replace immediately any furniture or effects lost damaged or destroyed and not to remove or permit to be removed any furniture or effects from the premises.

(v)   Not to make any alterations or additions to the premises without the consent of the Landlord.

(vi)   Not to carry on any business, trade or profession on or from the premises or receive any paying guests on the premises or use the premises otherwise than as a single *dwellinghouse/flat.

(vii)   Not to exhibit any notice or advertisement upon or near the premises or to do or permit to be done anything which may or shall cause nuisance, annoyance, inconvenience or disturbance to the Landlord or to any adjoining or neighbouring occupier.

(viii)   Not to assign, or sublet, part with possession of the premises or any part thereof.

(ix)   Not to keep any pets or animals on the premises or any part thereof.

(x)   To permit the Landlord or his authorised agent to enter on the premises at all reasonable times in order to examine the state of condition thereof and with reasonable notice to carry out works of maintenance or repair.

(xi)   To preserve and maintain the general character of the garden in a reasonable manner according to the season and not to cut down, lop or remove any tree, shrub or plants growing on or near the premises.

(xii) To yield up the premises at the expiration or sooner determination of the tenancy together with all the said furniture and effects in the same clean state of condition as they shall be in at the commencement of the tenancy.

4. The Tenant further agrees to deposit with the Landlord/his agent the sum of £   to be held against dilapidations, breakages, unpaid accounts, incidental costs for which the Tenant may be liable under this Agreement so that the deposit or any balance thereof shall be refunded to the Tenant on termination of the tenancy, but shall not be treated as rent or relieve the Tenant of the obligation to make full payments of rent.

5. THE LANDLORD AGREES with the Tenant as follows:

(1) Provided the Tenant shall pay the rent and perform the agreements on his part hereinbefore referred to, the Landlord shall permit the Tenant to have quiet enjoyment of the premises without lawful interruption by the Landlord or his agent.

(2) To pay all rates in respect of the premises save for all charges for gas, electricity and telephone.

6. If the rent shall remain unpaid for more than 14 days after the same has become due (whether legally demanded or not) or if the Tenant shall fail to observe or perform any of the stipulations contained in paragraph 3 hereof it shall be lawful for the Landlord to re-enter upon the premises and the tenancy hereby created shall come to an end without prejudice to any rights of action for arrears of rent or damages in respect of any breach of this Agreement.

AS WITNESS the hands of the said parties hereto the day and year first above written.

SIGNED by the above named

*Landlord/Tenant in the   [*Landlord/Tenant signs here*]
presence of:

[*Witness signs here,
giving address and occupation*]

*Delete where inapplicable

Schedule

FURNITURE AND EFFECTS LET WITH THE PREMISES
[leave a good space here for inventory]

---

3. Forms under the Housing Act 1988

(a) Prescribed information to be contained in a rent book

A tenant who pays rent weekly and who is an assured tenant, an assured shorthold tenant or an assured agricultural occupant must be given a rent book which contains the notice set out below. Any other weekly tenant is also entitled to a rent book and must be given certain information (see Chapter 1).

IMPORTANT – PLEASE READ THIS

If the rent for the premises you occupy as your residence is payable weekly, the landlord must provide you with a rent book or similar document. If you have an assured tenancy, including an assured *shorthold* tenancy (*see* paragraph 7 below), or an assured agricultural occupancy, the rent book or similar document must contain this notice, properly filled in.

1. Address of premises ....

*2. Name and address of landlord ....

*3. Name and address of agent (if any) ....

*4. The rent payable including/excluding † rates is £...... per week.

5. Details of accommodation (if any) which the occupier has the right to share with other persons.

....

* *These entries must be kept up-to-date.*
† *Cross out whichever does not apply.*

6. The other terms and conditions of the tenancy are ....
....

7. If you have an assured tenancy or an assured agricultural occupancy you have certain rights under the Housing Act 1988. These include the right not to be evicted from your home unless your landlord gets a possession order from the courts. Unless the property is let under an assured *shorthold* tenancy, the courts can only grant an order on a limited number of grounds. Further details regarding assured tenancies are set out in the Department of the Environment and Welsh Office booklet "Assured Tenancies" no 19 in the series of housing booklets. These booklets are available from rent officers, council offices and housing aid centres, some of which also give advice.

8. You may be entitled to get help to pay your rent and rates through the housing benefit scheme. Apply to your local council for details.

9. It is a criminal offence for your landlord to evict you without an order from the court or to harass you or interfere with your possessions or use of facilities in order to force you to leave.

10. If you are in doubt about your legal rights or obligations, particularly if your landlord has asked you to leave, you should go to a Citizens' Advice Bureau, housing aid centre, law centre or solicitor. Help with all or part of the cost of legal advice from a solicitor may be available under the Legal Aid Scheme.

The remaining forms in this Appendix are prescribed by the Assured Tenancies and Agricultural Occupancies (Forms) Regulations 1988 and should always follow the set wording.

(b) *Notice proposing different terms for statutory periodic tenancy*

When a fixed term assured or assured shorthold tenancy comes to an end and the tenant remains in possession of the property as a statutory periodic tenant, this form can be used by either the landlord or the tenant to alter the terms of the tenancy. It must be served within a year of the ending of the fixed term tenancy.

Housing Act 1988 section 6(2)

Notice Proposing Different Terms for Statutory Periodic Tenancy

- Please write clearly in black ink.

- **This notice proposes changes to the terms of the statutory periodic tenancy. If you wish to refer it to a rent assessment committee you must keep to the time limit set out in paragraph 2 below.**

- It can be used by either a landlord or a tenant.

- This notice must be served no later than the first anniversary of the day after the former fixed term tenancy or occupancy ended.

- Do not use this notice if you are a landlord only proposing an increase in rent.

- Please read this notice very carefully as it may alter the terms of the statutory periodic tenancy which arises when a fixed term assured tenancy runs out. It may also be used when a fixed term assured agricultural occupancy ends.

- If you need help or advice about this notice, and what you should do about it, take it immediately to any of the following:

- a Citizens' Advice Bureau,

- a housing aid centre,

- a law centre or a solicitor.

1. To:

      Name(s) of landlord(s) or tenant(s)★

of:

      Address of premises

2. This is to give notice that I/we★ propose different terms of the statutory periodic tenancy from those in the fixed term assured tenancy which has now ended to take effect from

          19

This date must be at least three months after this notice is served.

★*Cross out whichever does not apply.*

- If you agree with the new terms and rent proposed, do nothing. They will become the terms of your tenancy agreement on the date specified in paragraph 2.

- If you don't agree with the proposed terms and any adjustment of the rent (see paragraph 4), and you are unable to reach agreement with your landlord/tenant, or you do not wish to discuss it with him, you may refer the matter directly to your local rent assessment committee, **within three months of the date on which the notice was served,** using a special form.

- The committee will determine the proposed changes in the terms of the tenancy or some other different terms covering the same points, and the appropriate level of rent, if this applies.

3. Changes to the terms

   (a) the provisions of the tenancy to be changed are —
     *Please attach relevant sections of the agreement
     if available.*

   (b) The proposed changes are —
     (*Continue on a separate sheet if necessary.*)

4.★ Changes to the rent, if applicable
   The existing rent is   £   per
                         e.g. week, month, year
   This includes rates★

   The new rent which takes into account
   the proposed changes in the terms of the tenancy
   will be —   £   per
                         e.g. week, month, year
   This includes rates★

- Changes to the rent are optional. A proposal to adjust the rent to take account of the proposed new terms at paragraph 3 may be made if either the landlord or the tenant considers it appropriate.

To be signed by the landlord or his agent (someone acting for him) or the tenant or his agent. If there are joint landlords or joint tenants each landlord/ tenant or the agent must sign unless one signs on behalf of the rest with their agreement.

Signed:

Name(s) of landlord(s)/tenant(s):

Address of landlord(s)/tenant(s):

Tel:

If signed by agent, name and address of agent

Tel: *Date:*

*Cross out if this does not apply.

(c) Application referring a notice under section 6(2) to a rent assessment committee

If either a landlord or tenant has served notice to alter the terms of a statutory periodic tenancy, this form should be used to refer the notice to a rent assessment committee. They will decide whether the terms of the tenancy should be altered, and if so, whether a new rent should be fixed.

Housing Act 1988 section 6(3)

Application Referring a Notice Under Section 6(2) to a Rent Assessment Committee

- Please write clearly in black ink.

- Please tick boxes where appropriate.

- When you have filled in the form please send it to the appropriate rent assessment panel.

- Make sure you also send a copy of the notice served on you proposing the new terms of the statutory periodic tenancy.

- This application may be used by a landlord or a tenant who has been served with a notice under section 6(2) of the Housing Act 1988, varying the terms of a statutory periodic tenancy. It may also be used where there was an earlier assured agricultural occupancy.

1. Address of premises

2. Name(s) of tenant(s)

3. Name(s) of landlord(s)

   Address of landlord(s)

4. Details of premises.
   (a) What type of property is it, eg house, flat or room(s)?

   (b) If it is a flat or room(s) say what floor(s) it is on.

   (c) Give the number and type of rooms, eg living room, bathroom.

   (d) Does the tenancy include any other facilities, eg garden, garage or other separate building or land?   Yes ☐ No ☐

   (e) If Yes, please give details.

   (f) Is any of the accommodation shared?

      (i) with the landlord?   Yes ☐ No ☐

      (ii) with another tenant or tenants?   Yes ☐ No ☐

   (g) If Yes, please give details.

5. What is the current rateable value of the premises? £

6. When did the statutory tenancy begin?   19

7. Services

   (a) Are any services provided under the tenancy (eg cleaning, lighting, heating, hot water or gardening)?   Yes ☐ No ☐

   (b) If Yes, please give details.

   (c) Is a separate charge made for services, maintenance, repairs, landlord's costs of management or any other item?   Yes ☐ No ☐

   (d) What charge is payable?   £

   (e) Does the charge vary according to the relevant costs?
                                                               Yes ☐ No ☐

   (f) If Yes, please give details.

8. (a) Is any furniture provided under the tenancy?   Yes ☐ No ☐

   (b) If Yes, please give details
   (*continue on a separate sheet if necessary*).

9. What repairs are the responsibility of

   (a) the landlord?

   (b) the tenant?
   (*continue on a separate sheet if necessary*).

10. (a) Give details of the other terms of the tenancy, eg whether the tenancy is assignable and whether a premium may be charged on an assignment
    (*continue on a separate sheet if necessary*).

    (b) Please attach the tenancy agreement (or a copy), with a note of any variations, if you have one. It will be returned to you without delay.

11. I/We* attach a copy of the notice proposing changes to the statutory periodic tenancy and, if applicable, an adjustment of the amount of rent and apply to the rent assessment committee to consider it.

Cross out whichever does not apply.

To be signed by the landlord or his agent (someone acting for him), or by the tenant or his agent. If there are joint landlords or joint tenants each landlord/ tenant or the agent must sign, unless one signs on behalf of the rest with their agreement.

Signed:

Name(s) of landlord(s)/tenant(s):

Address of landlord(s)/tenant(s):

Tel:

If signed by agent, name and address of agent

Tel: *Date:*   *19*

(d) Notice seeking possession of a property let on an assured tenancy

A landlord *must* use this form of notice when seeking possession of property let on an assured tenancy. It is important to make sure that sufficient notice is given to a tenant and legal advice should be sought.

Housing Act 1988 section 8

Notice Seeking Possession of a Property Let on an Assured Tenancy

- Please write clearly in black ink.

- Do not use this form if possession is sought from an assured shorthold tenant under section 21 of the Housing Act 1988 or if the property is occupied under an assured agricultural occupancy.

- **This notice is the first step towards requiring you to give up possession of your home. You should read it very carefully.**

- If you need advice about this notice, and what you should do about it, take it as quickly as possible to any of the following –

  - a Citizens' Advice Bureau,

  - a housing aid centre,

  - a law centre,

  - or a solicitor.

You may be able to get Legal Aid but this will depend on your personal circumstances.

1. To: *Name(s) of tenant(s)*

2. Your landlord intends to apply to the court for an order requiring you to give up possession of —

(Address of premises)

- If you have an assured tenancy under the Housing Act 1988, which is not an assured shorthold tenancy, you can only be required to leave your home if your landlord gets an order for possession from the court on one of the grounds which are set out in Schedule 2 to the Act.

- If you are willing to give up possession of your home without a court order, you should tell the person who signed this notice as soon as possible and say when you can leave.

3. **The landlord intends to seek possession on ground(s) ...... in Schedule 2 to the Housing Act 1988, which reads**

   Give the full text of each ground which is being relied on. (Continue on a separate sheet if necessary.)

   ● Whichever grounds are set out in paragraph 3 the court may allow any of the other grounds to be added at a later date. If this is done, you will be told about it so you can discuss the additional grounds at the court hearing as well as the grounds set out in paragraph 3.

4. **Particulars of each ground are as follows –**

   Give a full explanation of why each ground is being relied. (Continue on a separate sheet if necessary.)

   ● If the court is satisfied that any of grounds 1 to 8 is established it must make an order (but see below in respect of fixed term tenancies).

   ● Before the court will grant an order on any of grounds 9 to 16, it must be satisfied that it is reasonable to require you to leave. This means that, if one of these grounds is set out in paragraph 3, you will be able to suggest to the court that it is not reasonable that you should have to leave, even if you accept that the ground applies.

   ● The court will not make an order under grounds 1, 3 to 7, 9 or 16, to take effect during the fixed term of the tenancy; and it will only make an order during the fixed term on grounds 2, 8 or 10 to 15 if the terms of the tenancy make provision for it to be brought to an end on any of these grounds.

   ● Where the court makes an order for possession solely on ground 6 or 9, your landlord must pay your reasonable removal expenses.

5. **The court proceedings will not begin until after   19**

   Give the date after which court proceedings can be brought.

   ● Where the landlord is seeking possession under grounds 1, 2, 5 to 7, 9 or 16 in Schedule 2, court proceedings cannot begin earlier than 2 months from the date this notice is served on you and not before the date on which the tenancy (had it not been served) could have been brought to an end by a notice to quit served at the same time as this notice.

- Where the landlord is seeking possession on grounds 3, 4, 8 or 10 to 15, court proceedings cannot begin until 2 weeks after the date this notice is served.

- After the date shown in paragraph 5, court proceedings may be begun at once but not later than 12 months from the date this notice is served. After this time the notice will lapse and a new notice must be served before possession can be sought.

To be signed by the landlord or his agent (someone acting for him).

Signed:

Names(s) of landlord(s):

Address of landlord(s):

Tel:

If signed by agent, name and address of agent:

Tel: *Date:*   *19*

(e) Landlord's notice proposing a new rent under an assured periodic tenancy or agricultural occupancy

This notice must be served by a landlord who wants to increase the rent of a periodic assured tenancy. It can be used to increase the rent of a statutory periodic tenancy but *not* where a change of terms is proposed, when the other form (see page 118) should be used. The increased rent cannot take effect any earlier than a year after the start of the tenancy, or a year from a previous determination of the rent by a rent assessment committee, and a period of between one and six months from the date of the notice. The form gives these minimum periods and they should be read carefully.

Housing Act 1988 section 13(2)

Landlord's Notice Proposing a New Rent Under An Assured Periodic Tenancy or Agricultural Occupancy

- Please write clearly in black ink.

- Do not use this form if there is a current rent fixing mechanism in the tenancy.

- Do not use this form to propose a rent adjustment for a statutory periodic tenancy solely because of a proposed change of terms under section 6(2) of the Housing Act 1988.

- This notice may also be used to propose a new rent or licence fee for an assured agricultural occupancy. In such a case references to "landlord"/"tenant" can be read as references to "licensor"/"licensee" etc.

- **This notice proposes a new rent. If you want to oppose this proposal you must keep to the time limit set out in paragraph 2.**

Read this notice carefully. If you need help or advice take it immediately to:

- a Citizens' Advice Bureau,

- a housing aid centre,

- a law centre,

- or a solicitor.

1. To: *Name(s) of tenant(s)*

   of: *Address of premises*

2. This is to give notice that as from   19
   your landlord proposes to charge a new rent.

   The new rent must take effect at the beginning of a new period of the tenancy and not earlier than any of the following –

   (a) the minimum period after this notice was served,
       (the minimum period is —

       - in the case of a yearly tenancy, six months,

       - in the case of a tenancy where the period is less than a month, one month, and

       - in any other case, a period equal to the period of the tenancy.)

(b) the first anniversary of the start of the first period of the tenancy except in the case of —

- a statutory periodic tenancy, which arises when a fixed term assured tenancy ends, or

- an assured tenancy which arose on the death of a tenant under a regulated tenancy,

(c) if the rent under the tenancy has previously been increased by a notice under section 13 or a determination under section 14 of the Housing Act 1988, the first anniversary of the date on which the increased rent took effect.

3. The existing rent is   £   per
                                                           eg. week, month, year

This includes/excludes* rates

4. The proposed new rent will be   £   per
                                                           eg. week, month, year

This includes/excludes* rates

Cross out whichever does not apply.

- If you agree with the new rent proposed do nothing. If you do not agree and you are unable to reach agreement with your landlord or do not want to discuss it directly with him, you may refer the notice to your local rent assessment committee before the beginning of the new period given in paragraph 2. The committee will consider your application and will decide whether the proposed new rent is appropriate.

- You will need a special form to refer the notice to a rent assessment committee.

To be signed by the landlord or his agent (someone acting for him). If there are joint landlords each landlord or his agent must sign unless one signs on behalf of the rest with their agreement.

Signed:

Name(s) of landlord(s):

Address of landlord(s):

Tel:

If signed by agent, name and address of agent:

Tel: *Date*   *19*

(f) Application referring a notice proposing a new rent under an assured periodic tenancy or agricultural occupancy to a rent assessment committee

Housing Act 1988 section 13(4)

Application Referring A Notice Proposing A New Rent Under An Assured Periodic Tenancy or Agricultural Occupancy to a Rent Assessment Committee

- Please write clearly in black ink.

- Please tick boxes where appropriate.

- When you have filled the form in please send it to the appropriate rent assessment panel.

- You should use this form when your landlord has served notice on you proposing a new rent under an assured periodic tenancy.

- You will need to attach a copy of that notice to this form.

- This form may also be used to refer a notice proposing a new rent or licence fee for an assured agricultural occupancy. In such a case references to "landlord"/"tenant" can be read as references to "licensor"/"licensee" etc.

1. Address of premises

2. Name(s) of landlord(s)

   Address of landlord(s)

3. Details of premises.

   (a) What type of property is it, eg house, flat or room(s)?

   (b) If it is a flat or room(s) say what floor(s) it is on.

   (c) Give the number and type of rooms, eg living room, bathroom.

   (d) Does the tenancy include any other facilities, eg garden, garage or other separate building or land?   Yes ☐ No ☐

   (e) If Yes, please give details.

   (f) Do you share any accommodation?

     (i) with the landlord?   Yes ☐ No ☐

     (ii) with another tenant or tenants?   Yes ☐ No ☐

   (g) If Yes to either of the above, please give details.

4. What is the current rateable value of the premises? £

5. (a) When did the present tenancy begin?   19

   (b) When does the present tenancy end?   19

6. (a) Did you pay a premium?   Yes ☐ No ☐

   (b) If Yes, please give details.

7. Services

   (a) Are any services provided under the tenancy (eg cleaning, lighting, heating, hot water or gardening)?   Yes ☐ No ☐

   (b) If Yes please give details.

   (c) Is a separate charge made for services, maintenance, repairs, landlord's costs of management or any other item?   Yes ☐ No ☐

   (d) What charge is payable?   £

   (e) Does the charge vary according to the relevant costs?   Yes ☐ No ☐

   (f) If Yes, please give details.

8. (a) Is any furniture provided under the tenancy?   Yes ☐ No ☐

(b) If Yes, please give details
(*continue on a separate sheet if necessary*).

9. Improvements

(a) Have you, or any former tenant(s) carried out improvements or replaced fixtures, fittings or furniture for which you or they were not responsible under the terms of the tenancy?   Yes ☐ No ☐

(b) If Yes, please give details
(*continue on a separate sheet if necessary*).

10. What repairs are the responsibility of

(a) the landlord?

(b) the tenant?
(*continue on a separate sheet if necessary*).

11. (a) Give details of the other terms of the tenancy, eg whether the tenancy is assignable and whether a premium may be charged on an assignment
(*continue on a separate sheet if necessary*).

(b) Please attach the tenancy agreement, or a copy (with a note of any variations), if you have one. It will be returned to you as quickly as possible.

12. Do you have an assured agricultural occupancy?   Yes ☐ No ☐

13. I/We* attach a copy of the notice proposing a new rent under the assured periodic tenancy and I/we* apply for it to be considered by a rent assessment committee.

To be signed by the tenant or his agent (someone acting for him). If there are joint tenants, each tenant or his agent must sign, unless one signs on behalf of the rest with their agreement.

Signed:

Name of tenant(s):

Address of tenant(s):

Tel:

If signed by agent, name and address of agent:

Tel: *Date:*   *19*

★Cross out whichever does not apply.

(g) *Notice of an assured shorthold tenancy*

This notice must be given *before* the start of an assured shorthold tenancy and it *must* be in this form. If not, a landlord will have great difficulty getting possession of the property.

Housing Act 1988 section 20

Notice of an Assured Shorthold Tenancy

- Please write clearly in black ink.

- If there is anything you do not understand you should get advice from a solicitor or a Citizens' Advice Bureau before you agree to the tenancy.

- The landlord must give this notice to the tenant before an assured shorthold tenancy is granted. It does not commit the tenant to take the tenancy.

- **This document is important, keep it in a safe place.**

To: *Name of proposed tenant. If a joint tenancy is being offered enter the names of the joint tenants.*

1. *You are proposing to take a tenancy of the dwelling known as:*

from   /   /19   to   /   /19   *The tenancy must be for a term*
day month year day month year   *certain of at least six months.*

2. This notice is to tell you that your tenancy is to be an assured shorthold tenancy. Provided you keep to the terms of the tenancy, you are entitled to remain in the dwelling for at least the first six months of the fixed period agreed at the start of the tenancy. At the end of this period, depending on the terms of the tenancy, the landlord may have the right to repossession if he wants.

3. The rent for this tenancy is the rent we have agreed. However, you have the right to apply to a rent assessment committee for a determination of the rent which the committee considers might reasonably be obtained under the tenancy. If the committee considers (i) that there is a sufficient number of similar properties in the locality let on assured tenancies and that (ii) the rent we have agreed is significantly higher than the rent which might reasonably be obtained having regard to the level of rents for other assured tenancies in the locality, it will determine a rent for the tenancy. That rent will be the legal maximum you can be required to pay from the date the committee directs.

4. This notice was served on you on   19

To be signed by the landlord or his agent (someone acting for him). If there are joint landlords each must sign, unless one signs on behalf of the rest with their agreement.

Signed

Name(s) of the landlord(s):

Address of landlord(s):

Tel:

If signed by agent, name and address of agent:

Tel: *Date:*   19

Special note for existing tenants

- Generally if you already have a protected or statutory tenancy and you give it up to take a new tenancy in the same or other accommodation owned by the same landlord, that tenancy cannot be an assured tenancy. It can still be a protected tenancy.

- But if you currently occupy a dwelling which was let to you as a protected shorthold tenancy, special rules apply.

- If you have an assured tenancy which is not a shorthold under the Housing Act 1988, you cannot be offered an assured shorthold tenancy of the same or other accommodation by the same landlord.

(h) Application to a rent assessment committee for a determination of a rent under an assured shorthold tenancy

Housing Act 1988 section 22(1)

Application to a Rent Assessment Committee for a Determination of a Rent Under an Assured Shorthold Tenancy

- Please write clearly in black ink.

- Please tick boxes where appropriate.

- A tenant with a fixed term assured shorthold tenancy may use this form to apply to the local rent assessment committee, during the fixed term, to have the rent reduced. This form cannot be used in the cases specified at the end of this form.

- The form may also be used to apply to have the rent reduced for a fixed term assured shorthold* tenancy which is an assured agricultural occupancy. In such a case, references to "landlord"/"tenant" can be read as references to "licensor"/"licensee" etc.

- When you have filled the form in please send it to the appropriate rent assessment panel.

[* *Readers should ignore the word "shorthold" here — this is a mistake on the form, and it is due for amendment by statutory instrument in due course.*]

1. Address of premises

2. Name(s) of landlord(s)

   Address of landlord(s)

3. Details of premises.

   (a) What type of property is it, eg house, flat or room(s)?

   (b) If it is a flat or room(s) say what floor(s) it is on.

   (c) Give the number and type of rooms, eg living room, bathroom etc.

(d) Does the tenancy include any other facilities, eg garden, garage or other separate building or land?   Yes ☐ No ☐

(e) If Yes, please give details.

(f) Do you share any accommodation?

  (i) with the landlord?   Yes ☐ No ☐

  (ii) with another tenant or tenants?   Yes ☐ No ☐

(g) If Yes to either of the above, please give details.

4. What is the current rateable value of the premises? £

5. (a) When did the present tenancy begin?   19

  (b) When does the present tenancy end?   19

6. (a) Please confirm by ticking box that you received   ☐
a notice saying that the tenancy was to be an assured shorthold tenancy before the agreement was entered into.

  (b) Attach a copy of the notice if available.
It will be returned without delay.

7. (a) Did you pay a premium?   Yes ☐ No ☐

  (b) If Yes, please give details.

8. Services
  (a) Are any services provided under the tenancy (eg cleaning, lighting, heating, hot water or gardening)?   Yes ☐ No ☐

  (b) If Yes, please give details.

  (c) Is a separate charge made for services, maintenance, repairs, landlord's costs of management or any other item?   Yes ☐ No ☐

  (d) What charge is payable?   £

  (e) Does the charge vary according to the relevant costs?
   Yes ☐ No ☐

  (f) If Yes, please give details.

9. (a) Is any furniture provided under the tenancy?   Yes ☐ No ☐

   (b) If Yes, please give details
       (*continue on a separate sheet if necessary*).

10. What repairs are the responsibility of

    (a) the landlord?

    (b) the tenant?
        (*continue on a separate sheet if necessary*).

11. (a) Give details of the other terms of the tenancy, eg whether the tenancy is assignable and whether a premium may be charged on an assignment
        (*continue on a separate sheet if necessary*).

    (b) Please attach the tenancy agreement, or a copy (with a note of any variations) if you have one. It will be returned to you as quickly as possible.

12. The existing rent is   £   per
                                        eg, week, month, year
    This includes/excludes* rates of   £   per

13. I/We* apply to the rent assessment committee to determine a rent for the above mentioned premises.

To be signed by the tenant or his agent (someone acting for him). If there are joint tenants, each tenant or his agent must sign, unless one signs on behalf of the rest with their agreement.

Signed:

Name of tenant(s):

Address of tenant(s):

Tel:

If signed by agent, name and address of agent:

Tel: *Date:*   19

*Cross out whichever does not apply.

- An application cannot be made if –
  (a) the rent payable under the tenancy is a rent previously determined by a rent assessment committee; or

  (b) the tenancy is an assured shorthold tenancy that came into being on the ending of a tenancy which had been an assured shorthold of the same, or substantially the same, property and the landlord and tenant under each tenancy were the same at the time.

- the rent assessment committee cannot make a determination unless it considers –

  (a) that there is a sufficient number of similar dwelling-houses in the locality let on assured tenancies (whether shorthold or not); and

  (b) that the rent payable under the shorthold tenancy in question is significantly higher than the rent which the landlord might reasonably be expected to get in comparison with other rents under the assured tenancies mentioned in (a) above.

Appendix 2

House Rules

As suggested on page 85, owners who take lodgers into their homes are advised to prepare a set of House Rules. The example given below can be adapted as appropriate to the particular case. For instance, an owner might wish to add a rule to the effect that the deposit will be lost if furniture or equipment is damaged. When giving a receipt for the deposit, the owner should give the guest a copy of the House Rules and ask the guest to sign them.

1. The price for the use of the room [with breakfast [and evening meal]] is £...... per week, payable every Friday. (*Alternatively, for example, the price might be quoted for bed and breakfast Monday to Friday with full board at weekends.*)

2. The room will be cleaned and the sheets changed once a week. The guest is asked to keep the room tidy at all times.

3. Overnight guests are not permitted.

4. Guests are asked not to play loud music or to cause annoyance or nuisance to the owner or any other occupier.

5. Guests share the bathroom and kitchen, and are requested to leave both rooms clean and tidy after use.

6. Guests will be given seven days' notice to leave, but the owner may give earlier notice if he so wishes.

7. Guests may use the lounge at the owner's invitation.

8. Guests have the use of a bedroom assigned by the owner, but do not have exclusive possession.

9. Pets are not allowed on the premises.

10. Guests are asked not to re-arrange the furniture or to fix posters, pictures or anything else to the walls without the prior consent of the owner.

Appendix 3

Model brochure and letters for holiday lettings

As explained in Chapter 4, a short but attractive brochure will help immeasurably in attracting bookings for a holiday home. Page 57 gives suggestions about how to go about arranging the printing. A suitable brochure might consist of four pages; the first showing the name of the property and a photograph or drawing; the last page giving a local map. The inner two pages contain details of the accommodation, rental and so on. For example:

Set close to the village centre in a quiet backstreet yet backing onto open countryside, Honeysuckle Cottage is ideally suited for those who enjoy the delights of walking, as well as for those who wish to tour the Cotswolds.

The nearby Cotswold market town of Loose Chippings (pop. 7,000) encompasses all that is normally associated with this delightful area in the heart of England, quaint old inns, well established shops, a beautiful Norman Church and many delightful walks.

Honeysuckle Cottage consists of the following:

Entrance Porch leading to —

Kitchen	fully modernised and equipped, electric cooker, fridge, etc, with utensils for 6 guests.
Lounge/Diner	quite spacious and very comfortably, furnished, with open inglenook fire place and colour T.V.
Upstairs	2 double bedrooms, one with double bed, and one twin bedded, with one small bedroom containing bunk beds.
Bathroom	Bath, W.C., washbasin and airing-cupboard.

Carpeting throughout. A washing machine is available and there are ample car parking facilities.

Where to find Honeysuckle Cottage: Having entered
the village on the A123 go into the village centre,
turn down the small lane to the side of the Post
Office. Follow the road round to the right,
Honeysuckle Cottage is set back a little, approx 200
yards from the Post Office.

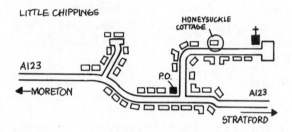

Terms of Hire: The cottage is available on a
minimum weekly basis from one Saturday to the
next: you may of course have as many weeks as you
like from:

April to June at £   .   per week
July to September at £   .   per week
October to March at £   .   per week

Electricity is by 50p coin meter and storage heaters
are included in the rent.

When booking please forward £   .   deposit and
the remaining balance on your arrival.

John Smith
The Old Smithy
Loose Chippings
Worcestershire
Tel: 0123-45678

Draft letters

The standard letters set out below can be typed out with appropriate modifications and photocopied to provide a small stock. The name and address of the person inquiring can then be filled in, and the date inserted, as the letters are used. By using photocopied standard letters in this way, much time can be saved, and sending out a "booking letter" will certainly encourage bookings.

Letter 1: *Owner's address and phone no.:*
Date:

Dear

Honeysuckle Cottage

Thank you for your enquiry in connection with the above cottage. I am pleased to enclose a brochure detailing the position of the cottage, its accommodation and the terms. I am also enclosing a letter of confirmation for you to sign should you wish to make a booking.

If there is anything further you require to know about the property or its availability please telephone me.

Yours

Letter 2: From:

Dear

Honeysuckle Cottage

I write to confirm my booking of Honeysuckle Cottage from Saturday the   to Saturday   19   at a total cost of £   .

I enclose a cheque in the sum of £   . by way of a deposit for this booking.

Yours

Note: Letter 2 is a pro-forma letter which should be sent out to each enquirer with a brochure. Once completed, signed and returned to the owner, together with a deposit, the letter confirms the booking and is evidence of a binding contract. It is advisable to send such a letter as the terms of the booking are confirmed as well as encouraging a reply.

The deposit should be at least 25% of the total amount due.

Letter 3:   *Owner's address and phone no.:*
                                 Date:

Dear

Honeysuckle Cottage

Thank you for your letter and cheque in the sum of
£   .   which I accept as a deposit.
    I am pleased to confirm your booking from Saturday
            to Saturday   19   .
EITHER
I look forward to meeting you on your arrival at
Honeysuckle Cottage between 2pm and 3pm on the
        [*date of arrival*]. If you are likely to be much later
please let me know.
OR
The key will be left with Mrs Helpful at 1 Meadow View
(Tel: 0123-45679) who lives opposite Honeysuckle
Cottage and who will be pleased to show you to the
cottage and answer any queries. Mrs Helpful will expect
to see you between 2pm and 3pm on the   [*date of
arrival*] but if you are likely to arrive much later please let
her know.
    I hope that you enjoy your stay.

Yours

Index